MURTY CLAS

LIBRARY OF INDIA

GURU NANAK

POEMS FROM THE SIKH SACRED TRADITION

GURU NANAK

POEMS FROM THE SIKH SACRED TRADITION

Translated by
NIKKY-GUNINDER KAUR SINGH

MURTY CLASSICAL LIBRARY OF INDIA
HARVARD UNIVERSITY PRESS
Cambridge, Massachusetts
London, England
2023

First published in Murty Classical Library of India,
Volume 33, Harvard University Press, 2022.

SERIES DESIGN BY M9DESIGN

Library of Congress Cataloging-in-Publication Data

Names: Nānak, Guru, 1469-1538. Works. Selections. |
Nānak, Guru, 1469-1538. Works. Selections. English. |
Singh, Nikky-Guninder Kaur, translator.
Title: Poems from the Guru Granth Sahib / Guru Nanak ;
translated by Guninder Kaur Singh.
Other titles: Ādi-Granth. Selections English. | Ādi-Granth.
Description: Cambridge, Massachusetts :
Harvard University Press, 2022. |
Series: Murty classical library of India | Includes bibliographical
references | Introduction and notes in English. |
Identifiers: LCCN 2021014845 | ISBN 9780674290181 (pbk.)
Subjects: LCSH: Sikh poetry, Panjabi. |
Sikhism. | Religious poetry, Panjabi.
Classification: LCC BL2017.4 .A32 2022 | DDC 294.6/82--dc23
LC record available at https://lccn.loc.gov/2021014845

CONTENTS

CONTENTS

INTRODUCTION

Guru Nanak

Panjab—a region resounding with the songs of Bhagats and Sufis, lovers of god from various Indic and Islamic traditions—was the birthplace of Guru Nanak, founder of the Sikh religion, in 1469. He died there in 1539. His vast literary corpus—974 hymns recorded in the Guru Granth Sahib (GGS), the scripture of the Sikhs—embodies his pluralistic vision of the singular divine (*ikka*) in a multi-ethnic, multi-linguistic, and multi-religious world.

Although historical documentation on Guru Nanak is largely lacking, his life story is deeply imprinted in the collective memory of the Sikhs. Basic sources for his biography include scripture; the works of the earliest Sikh theologian, Bhai Gurdas (1551-1636); and popular stories about Guru Nanak's birth and life that began to circulate shortly after his death. Many of these quasi-mythic stories shaped and crystallized his core values for future generations.[1]

Our sources uniformly portray Guru Nanak as a spiritual person who was born into the Khatri mercantile community in the village of Talvandi (now in Pakistan), married Sulakhni, and had two sons. He was close to his older sister Nanaki. After her marriage he even lived in her home in Sultanpur Lodi, where he worked for the Muslim governor. In Sultanpur he experienced a religious revelation and traveled far beyond the Panjab with his Muslim companion, Bhai Mardana, visiting sacred sites and meeting with diverse groups of siddhas, Hindus, Muslims, Buddhists, Buddhists, and Jains. While Bhai Mardana strummed on his *rabab* (stringed instrument), a divinely inspired Nanak burst into song. Bhai Gurdas describes Guru Nanak as carrying a small volume with him, most likely a manuscript of his own hymns.[2] Eventually, Guru Nanak established a town named Kartarpur on the banks of the Ravi River, where he settled. The men and women who gathered there to hear and sing his sublime poetry and to practice the values of equality, civic action, and inclusivity formed the first Sikh community.

Guru Nanak was fully conscious of the novelty of his message and practice, and therefore sought to build an infrastructure that would provide momentum for later generations. Before his death he appointed his disciple Lahina as successor: he gave Lahina his book of verse and named him Angad, a limb (*anga*) of his body.[3]

A bodily link with poetry is underscored in several biographical stories about Guru Nanak. In one, he is bathing with a jug of water and watched by Guru Angad.[4] Pointing to a blue-black patch of skin on his ribcage, Guru Nanak explains to his future successor that, the night before, while a young shepherd was reciting his hymns on ground covered with thorny bushes, Nanak was accidentally bruised brushing against them. The porous nature of Guru Nanak's body— its fusion with his intangible word—strikingly conveys his physical presence in his verses. In a memorable illustration from the late nineteenth century, Guru Nanak is wearing an outfit with verses from the GGS and the holy Qur'an inscribed all over the front and sleeves.[5] Word and image present the first Sikh Guru effacing divisions: between himself and his poetry, Sikh and Muslim, body and spirit, language and reality, the temporal and the timeless.

The Guru Granth Sahib

Sikhs revere the Guru Granth Sahib—which translates literally as "the honored Guru in book form"—as the embodiment of their gurus. The sacred book constitutes the core of their ethics, philosophy, and aesthetics. It presides at all their ceremonies, rituals, and worship.

Guru Nanak's nine successors, the living gurus from Guru Angad (1504–1552) to Guru Gobind Singh (1666–1708), carried on his spiritual legacy. The second Guru added his writings to the ones he inherited and passed them on to the next. With the third, Guru Amar Das (1479–1574), there is evidence of a sacred anthology in the making: two volumes in the Gurmukhi script created under his supervision in the town of Goindval are still extant.[6] For his successor, Guru Amar Das chose his daughter Bibi Bhani's husband, Ram Das (1534–1581), who continued to compose hymns and foster the self-consciousness of the Sikhs. Their son Arjan (1563–1606), the poetically accomplished fifth Guru, produced the authoritative collection that has become known as the Guru Granth Sahib.

Since the fellowship of Sikhs had increased and spread geographically from the early days of Guru Nanak, a central canon was needed to guide their spiritual and moral life. Guru Arjan made selections from the works of the preceding four gurus, from his own expansive repertoire, and from the compositions of Hindu and Muslim saints that were part of his broader South Asian heritage. With Bhai Gurdas as his scribe, Guru Arjan methodically compiled a single text—known as the Kartarpur volume—that was ceremoniously installed in 1604 in a specially constructed building, the Golden Temple in Amritsar.[7] Based on it, the tenth Guru, Gobind Singh, prepared the Damdami volume that added the hymns of the ninth Guru, his father, Guru Tegh Bahadur (1621–1675). This is the final canonical version of the GGS.[8] The tenth teacher ended the line of succession by investing the role of guru in the scripture itself.[9]

This textual corpus contains not only the verses of the Sikh Gurus but also those of several Hindu and Muslim holy men. Here we find one of the earliest compilations of Kabir's poems, as well as the earliest extant example of Panjabi poetry by Shaikh Farid, one of the founders of the popular Chishti Sufi order in India.[10] The compositions span five centuries and represent regions across the Indian subcontinent. Various authors exalt the divine One in a kaleidoscope of images, allusions, and symbols; they also offer compelling critiques of the ancient caste system, untouchability, religious divisions, and basic human degradation. The GGS serves as an important historical archive, bringing together a range of religions, cultures, ethnicities, languages, and musical measures.

Guru Nanak's Poetry and Philosophy

Guru Nanak identifies himself as a poet. The singular reality is acknowledged as the source of his voice, his sensibility, his very being: "My breath and flesh are totally yours, you are my absolute love; says the poet (*sāiru*) Nanak, you are our true provider."[11] In a state of perpetual longing for the infinite One, he describes himself as spiritually intoxicated: inebriated (*divānā*), impetuous (*betālā*), crazy (*baurānā*). Plato may have banished the poets from his republic, but the divinely inspired Guru tried to awaken his followers and revitalize their senses, psyche, imagination, and spirit through poetry. For the eminent Sikh scholar Harbans Singh, "His genius was best expressed in the poetical attitude. No other way would have been adequate to the range and depth of his mood."[12] Guru Nanak's literary genius lies in his ability to express profound metaphysical concepts in pithy and plain diction.

Guru Nanak's language is archaic Panjabi that draws upon a variety of regional languages and local dialects. Besides Siraiki, the language of southwestern Panjab, and old Khari Boli, the language of the Delhi region and the basis of modern Hindi and Urdu, Guru Nanak abundantly utilizes vocabulary drawn from Persian, Sanskrit, and Arabic. Christopher Shackle has called this language "the sacred language of the Sikhs."[13] The works of Guru Nanak and his successors have come down in a script named Gurmukhi, literally "from the Guru's mouth." Gurmukhi can be traced back to the Landa mercantile shorthand, also called Mahajani, that Guru Nanak used as a youngster while working in shops and granaries. His immediate successor developed and standardized the script.

The process of writing has profound significance in Guru Nanak's philosophical worldview. It serves as an expression for the One, the all-embracing ontological principle: "You are the writing board, you are the pen, you are the writing on the board."[14] His "Alphabet on the Wooden Board" introduces the Gurmukhi alphabet. Arabic and Nagari alphabet acrostics were popular in his milieu, and most of the stanzas of Guru Nanak's acrostic begin with letters of Gurmukhi in the very form used today. The need for a special script demonstrates Guru Nanak's aspiration for a unique way to preserve his vision, and its importance among Sikhs parallels that of the Arabic script for the holy Qur'an among Muslims.

His wide-ranging works use different meters, rhymes, stanzas, and compositional styles. His basic poetic form is the *saloku* (*śloka* in Sanskrit), a rhyming couplet with sixteen syllables in each line, sometimes printed as four half-lines of eight syllables each. Guru Nanak does not follow the syllabic pattern rigidly and creates subtle and powerful shifts by using parallelism between the halves of a line.

Salokus combine into longer compositions such as *vārs*, popular Panjabi folk ballads depicting heroic events. Guru Nanak adapted the form's narrative style but transformed its historical battlefield setting into a metahistorical, spiritual sphere. Successor gurus adopted his model, and there are altogether twenty-two in the GGS. These *vārs* consist of multiple *salokus*, "lyrics" in this translation, and conclude with a *pauṛī*, "envoi" in this translation. A *pauṛī* (used generally for stanza, literally the "step" of a ladder) is a rhyming verse set that forms part of a sequence in a hymn, as in the thirty-eight *pauṛīs* of the "Morning Hymn."

Each *vār* in the GGS is attributed to a primary author, but includes *salokus* by the other gurus that interact with and build upon the main author's central themes. To signal their spiritual continuation, all authors signed their compositions "Nanak." Nevertheless, actual authorship in the GGS is clearly identified by the word *mahalā* (literally meaning "palace" or "section") and a numeral. *Mahalā* 1 indicates a composition by the first Guru, *mahalā* 2 by the second Guru, and so on. Most include a special verse that carries the central theme and ends with the word "pause" (*rahāu*), beckoning readers, singers, and listeners to halt and reflect on it. In this volume, *rahāus* are italicized.

With the exception of his "Morning Hymn," Guru Nanak's hymns in the GGS are based on the traditional Indian musical system of ragas.[15] Each raga evolved in a specific region and has its specific characteristics: a season prescribed for its singing, a time of the day, an emotional mood, and a particular cultural climate. Sometimes a variant or style of the raga is also indicated by the term *gharu* (literally, "house") followed by a numeral. Besides classical modes, Guru Nanak drew upon the beats of folk music, on popular tunes, and on devotional (*bhakti*) and Sufi forms. What matters most to him, though, is spiritual efficacy: "We may win acclaim singing ragas, but without the name our mind is false and corrupt," he says.[16]

His works form the thematic and stylistic blueprint for the GGS, exemplified by the anthology's opening poem "Morning Hymn." Its prologue celebrates the singular reality and its qualities—the root doctrine of Sikh thought and practice—asserted at the outset with the numeral one. Guru Nanak goes on to name the formless all-inclusive being "truth" (*satu/sacu*), an absolute expression of the unity shared across the celestial, terrestrial, and nether worlds.

The thirty-eight stanzas of this hymn portray the singular being as an all-embracing *becoming* that flows in the cosmos and seeps into the human world of motions and emotions.

Guru Nanak expresses his ontological, epistemological, aesthetic, ethical, and soteriological views through the five spheres: morality (*dharamu*), knowledge (*giānu*), beauty (*saramu*), action (*karamu*), and truth (*sacu*). A vast scene of limitless continents, constellations, and universes in the fifth sphere of truth (stanza 37) transitions to a small, bustling smithy (stanza 38). Here a minter with his anvil and hammer, bellows and fire, is crafting coins. The coin is identical with truth itself; the commercial product is an integral expression of metaphysical truth that is touched and seen and passed from hand to hand. This highly structured imaginative sweep is an exercise in daily practice of truth. Not doctrinal or abstract, truth is lived and enacted, something that is *done.*

Guru Nanak's aesthetic consists of hearing, singing, and rejoicing in the infinite ensemble of vibrations: individual (the heartbeat of every species), social (of every class, caste, ethnicity), and of the ever-expanding multiverse. After all, it is the singular divine who plays the stringed *kinguri* instrument in each heart.[17] His oeuvre hymns the glorious One, the common matrix across space and time. Cosmic melodies, natural sounds, musical instruments, and biological rhythms create sonorous arabesques in his works. Gods, sages, beautiful women, water, wind, fire, heroes, ascetics, jewels, species, continents, and constellations unite in aural and visual splendor. Peacocks, frogs, songbirds, serpents, fish, sparrows, ants, and deer are fully part of it. This verbal-musical symbiosis is intrinsic to Guru Nanak's worldview and his teaching.

His lyrics embracing the One as father, mother, brother, friend, lover, husband are echoed by his successors throughout the GGS: "You are our mother, father, near and far; you permeate each of us."[18] Particularly striking is Guru Nanak's maternal imagery, which celebrates the infinite One through gestation, birthing, and lactation.[19] He also offers exciting possibilities of relating sensuously with the transcendent One: the joy and the enjoyer, the bride in her wedding dress and the groom on the nuptial bed, the fisherman and the fish, the waters and the trap, the weight holding the net as well as the lost ruby swallowed by the fish.[20] Guru Nanak's paradoxes break conventional modes of thinking, and his metaphors expand human experience.

Vismādu (wondrous joy) is the abiding mood of Guru Nanak's wide-ranging corpus. In a passage from the "Ballad in the Melody of Hope," his astonishment rings over and over: "*vismādu rūpa vismādu raṅga . . . vismādu dharatī vismādu khāni* ("Wondrous the forms, wondrous all the hues . . . wondrous this earth, wondrous its species").[21] The boundless One is physically seen, heard, smelled, and felt in every bit of the finite world. As the boundaries of an entity collapse, the Guru's wonder moves on to the next, and so he stays perpetually inebriated: "You are One, but with so many forms, says Nanak, I just can't grasp your wonders."[22]

Guru Nanak also prescribes no rules, gives no doctrinal or epistemic system to follow; instead, he motivates listeners and readers to search for themselves, think about the choices they make, and perform actions mindfully. At the opening of "Morning Hymn" he names the One being as truth, but then asks: "How then to be truthful? How to break the wall of lies?" He questions, challenges, overturns assumptions, and provokes his readers to reassess. A pungent juxtaposition of images jolts readers from placid acceptance of moral codes of purity and pollution sanctioned by society for millennia: "If the outfit is stained with blood we call it polluted, and those who suck the blood of humans we call pure-minded?"[23] Wit and sarcasm enrich his interactive style.

Language from the economic and political spheres reinforces Guru Nanak's poetry. He does not separate religiosity from the material, the practical, or the public; there is nothing pejorative about business and trade. Commercial language—"principle," "profit," "loss," and so on—is extensive. Having worked in granaries, he uses that lexicon with familiarity and innate force. Importantly, he applies commercial participation equally to all members of society: "We are all peddlers of our merchant, the heavy-weight owner."[24] This upends the stratified caste system. Vaishyas (merchants and farmers) are not just a caste of entrepreneurs; we are all Vaishyas.

Throughout the GGS, the timeless One acts across the various tenses of time: "True in the beginning, true across the ages, true in the now also, Nanak: true forevermore."[25] Guru Nanak was fascinated with time, drawing attention to temporality and the role and responsibility of humans through time—cosmic, personal, historical, timeless. As we shall see later, he innovatively utilizes genres that were shared by devotional poets in North India in poems such as "The Hours," "The Days of the Lunar Month," and "Song of the Twelve Months."

The Selection

Guru Nanak's literary corpus is enormous, and my objective in the selection process has been to gather the range and depth of his voice. I also wanted to maintain the poetic sanctity of both the collective liturgical hymns and the *vārs*, and as a result a few compositions by his successors are included in the first two sections, in the same format as they appear in the original GGS text. Several of Guru Nanak's long and popular hymns are presented here in full: "Morning Hymn," "Alphabet on the Wooden Board," "Discourse with the Siddhas," "Song of the Twelve Months," "The Days of the Lunar Month," and "Ballad of Hope." Shorter poems with special motifs are also included, like "The Hours," "Songs of Mourning," "Verses on Emperor Babur," "The Graceless," and "The Graceful." This compilation should serve as a resource for the study of the first Guru's spirituality and literary style.

Section 1 contains Guru Nanak's hymns recited during morning and evening worship, going back to the daily practice established in the first Sikh community at Kartarpur. According to Bhai Gurdas, "In the morning *Japu* was recited, and in the evening *Āratī* and *Sohilā*."[26] Guru Nanak's "Morning Hymn," *Japujī* (*japu* meaning "recitation, repetition" + *jī*, a suffix of respect), metamorphoses chronological time into timeless ambrosia suggesting that the invigorated consciousness of early morning is kept perpetually alive. The liturgical hymns combine verses from different gurus and highlight the organic texture of Sikh scripture: through enjoined cadences of words and rhythm, a warm sense of kinship, and spiritual joy, the different gurus become one voice in the GGS.

"That Gate," recited during the reflective period of dusk, collects nine hymns in different ragas—four by Guru Nanak, three by Guru Ram Das, and two by Guru Arjan. This evening hymn begins by reprising, with slight differences, stanza 27 from "Morning Hymn."

The late evening hymn *Sohilā,* meaning "praise," is recited before going to bed and at the cremation ground when there is a death in the family. Paradoxically, Guru Nanak depicts the dark experienced in the cycle of human existence in Gauri Dipaki raga, or "Gauri of Light." With its wedding metaphors, the hymn synchronizes the polar rites of marriage and death. In public and private worship, it is recited as the physical text of the GGS is put to rest for the night, and its "worship" (*āratī*) segment is especially festive. At the Golden Temple in Amritsar, for instance, the *Āratī* sung by the congregation fills the air as the sacred book is carried in a gold and silver palanquin from the central shrine. The ceremonial opening of the book every morning and its closing at night celebrate time's constant change, movement, and succession.

Section 2 contains the "Ballad in the Melody of Hope." In many places of worship this composition has become a part of the daily morning liturgy. The rhythmically repeated chime of its moral guidelines directs the actions that singers and listeners do over the course of the day.

Section 3 comprises the "Discourse with the Siddhas" (*Siddha goṣṭi*), which recounts Guru Nanak's discourse (*goṣṭi*) with perfected yogis during his travels. Naths and the siddhas appear interchangeably here, though technically they were two different ascetic sects. The location of the dialogue, its time frame, and the speakers are not explicit; nevertheless, Guru Nanak's synchronization of time with the timeless One comes out robustly in this dialogical format. Taking on yogic diction, he invests the transient clothes of the yogis, their earrings, and the items they carry with everlasting spirituality.

Section 4 is a selection of Guru Nanak's thematic compositions. "The Hours" (*Pahare*) draws on a traditional poetic form based on the Indian time frame in which night and day were each divided into four quarters or watches (*paharu*). It charts chronological time through the passage of gestation, infancy, youth, and old age.

"The Days of the Lunar Month" (*Thitīṅ*) is a paean to the divine glory felt intensely each day of the month. It is composed in a poetic form based on the cycle of lunar days (*thiti*), distinct from solar days (*vāra*), proceeding from the first day of lunar fortnight to the night of the new moon.

His "Song of the Twelve Months" synthesizes the universal and personal dimensions of lived time through the psychological and spiritual journey of a young woman longing for her divine beloved over the twelve months of the year. This hymn is in the *barahmasa* (twelve months) genre, "one of the chief carriers of a shared poetic language of emotions and the seasons in North India."[27]

In his "Songs of Mourning," Guru Nanak movingly utilizes the folk genre of the dirge. Traditionally, dirges were sung by a chorus of women eulogizing the dead. The women would gather for several days of mourning at the house of the dead person and wail, beating their breasts and thighs. Guru Nanak asks readers to squarely confront and overcome the much-feared phenomenon and rejoice in the splendor of this world. His conclusion: "This world is sheer magic" because it is the maker's "infinite form."[28]

The four "Verses on Emperor Babur" bring attention to historical time. Guru Nanak lived through Emperor Babur's conquest of the relatively peaceful regime of the Lodi Sultans, and his establishment of the Mughal Empire in 1526. As Harbans Singh notes, these hymns by Guru Nanak are "unexcelled for their power of expression and moral keenness. His poetry has important social meaning. Nowhere else in contemporary literature are the issues of the medieval Indian situation comprehended with such clarity or presented in tones of greater urgency."[29]

The historically significant "Alphabet on the Wooden Board," as discussed earlier, traces the new Gurmukhi alphabet in which the GGS was recorded.

"The Graceless" and "The Graceful" express the two poles of the moral axis central to Guru Nanak's work, the *gurmukhi* and the *manmukhi*. The "guru-facing" (whose faces, or *mukha,* are turned to the guru), like a graceful woman, see, hear, breathe, and taste the presence of the timeless One. Like a graceless woman, those facing their self (*mana,* which in Panjabi means both mind and heart) have no feel for the universal One.

Section 5 includes a selection, drawn from the main body of the scriptural text, of Guru Nanak's compositions arranged according to the various ragas in which they are to be sung and played. The literary textures of his compositions are in harmony with their melodic systematization based on seasons and times of the day. In keeping with the musical measure, his hymns in Basant raga, for instance, bloom with the glory of the spring and celebrate the infinite One as a tiny bumblebee, delicious fruit, and lush vine—all at once.

Overall, Guru Nanak's literary repertoire demonstrates his abundant knowledge of texts, myths, ideologies, social codes, musical modes, and practices current in medieval North India, and these selections sample that vibrant spectrum. They convey his joyous exaltation of the wondrous One, his pathos at the devastation of Hindu and Muslim masses by Babur's men, his pungent critique of the dogmatic and the religious elites, and his sensuous feel for the transcendent divine in every finite form.

Poetry is universal, Aristotle said, and Guru Nanak's lyrical oeuvre with its pluralistic values, diction, genres, and styles calls for resonance within and among traditions. His timeless melodies intersect with concrete historical moments, and in today's society with its escalating divisions and polarizations, these poems can serve cultural, political, psychological, social, spiritual, and environmental needs. In a sad tone Guru Nanak wonders, "What can the poor Veda or Kateb do when nobody recognizes the singular One?"[30] "Veda" is his metonym for the entire Indic tradition, not just the Veda, but also the Puranas, the *śāstras,* and the *smṛtis.* The "Kateb" is its Islamic counterpart—the holy Qur'an and also the Tawrut (Torah), the Zabur (Psalms), and the Injil (Gospel). The problem of "inter" and "intra" religious conflicts does not lie in the texts but in us humans, who neither reflect on them nor recognize the singular One. This new translation of the Guru Granth Sahib will enable us to reflect and enjoy these polymorphous patterns and multifarious statements in "the language of infinite love—*bhākhiā bhāu apāru.*"[31]

The Translation

There has been a tendency in English translations to insert archaic phrases to extol and exalt the *ikka* (One) in ways that distort Guru Nanak's intimate relationships. His simple words pour out from the depths of his being to embrace the all-encompassing One. He typically uses the informal second person "you" (*tun*) with a force that dissolves all distance and otherness. It is important that a translation preserve the informality, immediacy, and intimacy of his voice.

Guru Nanak also addresses the One in a variety of names that were commonly used by his contemporaries. I retain them because they give us intimations of his frontierless imagination (their translation can be found in the Glossary). The Islamic words for the divine—Khuda, Allah, Rahim, Parvadagaru, Meharvana, Haqq, Kabir, Karim, Maula, Rabb, Sahib—seamlessly join with the highest Buddhist goal of nirvana, and with the Hindu terms Hari, Ram, Prabh (also Prabhu and Prabhi), Dharnidhar, Gobind, Murari, Madhoji, Narayana, Paramesaru, Pranadhara, Sriranga, and Vasudeva. Balancing these masculine titles from various religious traditions, Guru Nanak also addresses the divine as female—Ammali, Mae, Mata, Prabhi, Sahiba.

The divine names from the Hindu world often refer to incarnations, whereas for Guru Nanak they invariably designate the non-incarnate divine. His "Morning Hymn" explicitly rejects the doctrine of incarnation (stanza 5). Likewise, in his repertoire, Arabic-Persian names such as Allah, Khuda, or Rahim evoke the infinite One who rejoices within everybody, rather than the customary distant monotheistic godhead of Islam to whom all creatures must submit. For Guru Nanak, "nirvana" is an expression for the One overflowing everywhere, in contrast to its use in Buddhism, where it describes emptiness. Understanding the familiar divine names in Guru Nanak's works requires a conscious break from our preconceptions and intellectual habits, so that we may imagine afresh and enjoy their limitless kaleidoscopic horizon.

Guru Nanak's words overall have a very particular feel to them. *Ikka* (One), *satu/sacu* (truth), *nāmu* (name), *sabadu/śabadu* (sacred word), *bāṇī* (sacred verse), *guru* (enlightener/enlightenment), *amrita* (ambrosia), *raṅga* (color), *rasa* (juice), *ānandu* (bliss), and *anhadu* (unstruck) are multivalent, for each is endowed with endless semantic potential. They merge into one another and become synonyms. Each is the revelation of the ineffable One, each is the medium for making the One manifest, and each is a sensuous experience of that transcendent One. They share a fundamental similarity in that they are present in every body (*deha*) and in each and every heart (*ghaṭi ghaṭi*). Each integrates ontological, ethical, aesthetic, and soteriological dimensions. Truth is the identification and designation of the ontological One, and only by living a truthful life is truth attained.

To translate these multivalent terms is challenging; it also is difficult to convey the inclusivity of Guru Nanak's unequivocal *ikkoaṅkār*. For the formless supreme being I used gender-inclusive language, the pronoun "it," unless the reference specifically called for masculine pronouns. It is indeed hard to reproduce the elemental simplicity, musicality, and aesthetic efficacy of Guru Nanak's verse.

To compound matters, the source material is stylistically epigrammatic. Guru Nanak's style is extremely condensed. Since he rarely uses conjunctions and prepositions, his text creates hermeneutic complications. Often a simple numeral—one, two, three—is philosophically weighty. I have kept the simple numerals in the translation and confined their explanation to the notes and glossary. Likewise, recurring key terms such as "gaze," "court," "order," "will," "command," "writing," and "palace" are aligned with the infinite reality, so they carry complex meanings. Guru Nanak uses a very compressed style, often not providing his verb with a subject. In such cases, I have used the first personal plural (we) in my translation to maintain the universal scope of his message.

Acknowledgments

I am most grateful to Professor Sheldon Pollock for taking me on board, and for including the works of the first Sikh Guru in his visionary project of the Murty Classical Library of India. My special thanks to Professor Archana Venkatesan for reading my manuscript and giving me many excellent suggestions. My thanks to Chief Secretary of the SGPC Sardar Harcharan Singh, Dr. Kulbir Thind, Heather Hughes, and Sharmila Sen for their manifold support, and to my students at Colby College for their engaged conversations. For the profound joy of reading Guru Nanak's poetry, I am grateful to my parents and grandmother, who awoke my interest, and to my brother, who ensures I keep it alive. Thanks too to my resonant drone string, Harry, and to my pick-me-up Bela.

But I have no words to thank my editor Francesca Orsini. I dedicate this work to her. Francesca's inspiration and labor make the impossible possible.

NOTES

1   Guru Nanak's life is told in the *Janamsākhīs*. These have come down in a variety of renditions such as the Bala, Miharban, Adi, and Puratan. For a comprehensive study, see McLeod 1980.

2   Bhai Gurdas depicts Guru Nanak "with a book under his arm" (*Vār* I: 32). Early Sikh paintings show Guru Nanak with a small volume either held by him or placed beside him (Goswamy and Smith 2006: 19, 23, and 32). For a textual study of the volume associated with Guru Nanak, see P. Singh 2000: 32–34; Mann 2001: 37–40.

3   Bards Satta and Balvand depict Guru Nanak passing on his legacy to Angad (GGS: 966–967). Also Bhai Gurdas, *Vār* I: 45.

4   Illustration 56 of the *B-40 Janamsākhī* (dated 1733), and named after its accession number at the India Office Library. For the image see Hans 1987, for the *Janamsākhī* narrative see McLeod 1981, and for a fuller analysis of these texts see N. G. K. Singh 2013. The hymns *Āratī* and *Sohilā* can be found in "Daily Worship" here.

5   The painting is at the Government Museum and Art Gallery in Chandigarh, printed and discussed by Goswamy 2000: 38–39.

6   Mann 1997, *Goindval Pothis.*

7   For the overall formation of Sikh scripture and the editorial skills displayed by the fifth Guru, see P. Singh 2000, Mann 2001, and Kohli 1961.

8   McLeod 2005: 5.

9   For more details on the transference of guruship to the GGS, see N. G. K. Singh 2008: 157–176.

10   It is believed that Guru Nanak procured his compositions from the Shaikh's descendants. Some scholars question the identity of the author. For details see Macauliffe 1909: 357.

11   See GGS: 660.

12   H. Singh 1969: 215–216.

13   Shackle 1983. See also Shackle 1988: 101–109.

14   See GGS: 1291.

15   Guru Nanak does have a composition in Bihagara raga (GGS: 556), but since it is a *saloku* that is not typically sung, it is not considered a raga and, therefore, not included in that section of our text.

16   See GGS: 414.

17   Page 164.

18   See GGS: 818.

19   N. G. K. Singh 1993: 48–89.

20   Page 150.

21   Page 41.

22   See GGS: 356.

23   See GGS: 140.

24   See GGS: 155.

25   Page 3. This opening verse is the one inscribed on his robe along with the Islamic invocation *bismillāh ar-rahman ar-rahīm* in the painting discussed earlier (above n. 5).

26   Bhai Gurdas *Vār* I: 38.

27   Orsini 2018: 99–100.

28   Page 121.

29   H. Singh 1969: 206.

30   GGS: 1153.

31   Page 4.

Daily Worship

MORNING HYMN

There is only One. Truth by name.   1
    Creator Purakhu, without fear, without hate,
    timeless in form, unborn, self-existent,
    recognized by the guru's grace.

Recite[1]
True in the beginning, true across the ages,
true in the now,
    Nanak: true forever.

One thought cannot think, nor can a million thoughts,
Silence cannot silence, nor can unbroken adoration.
The hunger of the hungry does not go away,
    not by the wealth of the whole world.
A thousand clever tricks can become a million,
    but not even one goes with us at the end.
How then to be truthful?
    How to break the wall of lies?
Follow the will, says Nanak, written down for us.[2]

By the will all forms are created,   2
    what the will is no one can say.
By that will all life is formed, all are made great.

3

The will determines the high and the low,
    the will writes out joy and suffering.[3]
The will blesses some, others wander endlessly.
All exist within the will, nothing stands apart.
Nanak: who knows the will won't say I or me.[4]

3   Those filled with might sing of its might,
those seeing its signs sing of its bounty,
the virtuous sing of its glory,
deep thinkers sing of its knowledge.
Some sing of the One who molds the body and turns it to
    dust,
some sing of its giving and taking life,
some sing of how far it seems in the distance,
some sing of how closely it watches all, ever present.
Stories upon stories, no end to the stories,
told and retold by millions and millions.
The giver gives, receivers tire of receiving,
age upon age they devour the gifts.
The leader leads by way of the will,
free from care, is ever joyful, says Nanak.

4   The true Sahib, true by name,[5]
    speaks the language of infinite love.
They speak and ask, "Give us, please give,"
    and the giver keeps giving.
What can we offer so we behold the divine court?
What words can we speak to be held dear?
In the timeless dawn praise the true name. Dwell on it.

Our actions give us this garment, the body.
    The gaze of love leads to the gate of liberation.
Nanak: know it for what it is, all this is truth itself.

The One can't be molded or made,[6]   5
pure, absolute, only itself.
Serve and be honored.
Nanak: sing of that treasure of virtues,
sing, listen, and hold love in your heart,
for sorrow is banished and joy enters.
Through the guru comes the numinous sound,[7]
    through the guru comes knowledge of the Vedas,
    through the guru the One is experienced in all.
The guru is Shiva, the guru is Vishnu, the guru is Brahma,[8]
    the guru is Parvati, Lakshmi, and Sarasvati.[9]
Were I to grasp it I'd still fail to explain
    the One beyond all telling.
The guru granted me one insight—
all living beings have the one giver,
    I must never forget.

I would bathe at a pilgrimage ford if it pleased the One,   6
    why bathe otherwise?
This entire span of creation I see
    couldn't exist without good deeds.
Hear a single teaching from the guru,
    and the mind shines with jewels, rubies, and pearls.
The guru gave me one insight—
all living beings have the one giver,
    I must never forget.

7 Were we to live through the four ages, or even ten times
        four,
    were we known in the nine realms, hailed as leaders by all,
    winning good name, glory, and fame across the world,
    but were denied the gaze of love, we'd be cast out,
    we'd be the lowest of worms, accused as the worst
        criminals.
    Nanak: the One gives virtues to those who lack them, and
        to the virtuous gives even more.
    That one of us could give virtue to the One is beyond
        thought.

8 Listening, we become like siddhas, naths, and *pīrs*,[10]
    listening, we fathom the earth, the underworld, and skies,
    listening, we know the nine continents, the many worlds
        and underworlds,
    listening, death can't come near us.
    Nanak: the devout enjoy bliss forever,
    listening removes all suffering and evil.

9 Listening, we become like Shiva, Brahma, and Indra,
    listening makes the corrupt open their mouths in praise,
    listening reveals yoga discipline and the body's mysteries,
    listening shines light on the shastras, smritis, and Vedas.
    Nanak: the devout enjoy bliss forever,
    listening removes all suffering and evil.

10 Listening leads to truth, contentment, knowledge,
    listening bathes us in the sixty-eight sacred sites,

listening wins scholarly fame,
listening inspires serene focus.
Nanak: the devout enjoy bliss forever,
listening removes all suffering and evil.

Listening, we plumb the depths of virtues,   11
listening, we rise to the status of *shaikhs, pīrs,* and kings,
listening, the blind find their way,
listening, our hands touch the unfathomable.
Nanak: the devout enjoy bliss forever,
listening removes all suffering and evil.

No words can tell the state of embracing,[11]   12
try explaining it and you'll regret later.
No paper, no pen, no scribe can describe it,
philosophizing is no help to realize it.
So wondrous is the stainless name,
only those who embrace it in their mind know it.

Embracing   13
        our mind and intellect awaken,
embracing
        we learn of all the worlds,
embracing
        our face is safe from blows,
embracing
        we part company with death.
So wondrous is the stainless name,
only those who embrace it in their mind know it.

14　Embracing
　　　we walk on a clear path,
　embracing
　　　we advance in honor and glory,
　embracing
　　　we don't stray down lanes and byways,
　embracing
　　　we bond with righteousness.
　So wondrous is the stainless name,
　only those who embrace it in their mind know it.

15　Embracing
　　　we find the door to liberation,
　embracing
　　　we liberate our family too,
　embracing
　　　we swim and carry the guru's learners across,
　embracing, says Nanak,
　　　we need not beg around.
　So wondrous is the stainless name,
　only those who embrace it in their mind know it.

16　The five win approval, the five are the leaders,[12]
　they receive honors at court,
　shine splendidly at the royal gates,
　attend to the only guru.
　However much we speak or think,
　the creator's doings are beyond calculation.
　The bull that bears the earth is righteousness, child of
　　　compassion,

its rope is contentment holding the earth in balance.
We will live truthfully once we realize
how heavy a weight the bull bears,
for there is not one earth but many more, above and
    beyond—
who stands beneath supporting them all?
The names of living beings, their varieties and colors,
were all written in a single pen stroke.
Were one to write this writ,
what endless writ it would be.
What power, beauty of form,
how great a gift—how to assess it?
This wide expanse from a single command,
from it a million rivers flew forth.
How to fathom or express this creative power?
I cannot offer myself to you even once,
only that which pleases you is good.
You are forever constant, formless One.

Countless are the ways of meditation,   17
    countless the avenues of love,
countless the ways of worship,
    countless the prayers and penances.
Countless texts and Vedic reciters,
countless yogis who turn from the world.
Countless the devout reflecting on virtue and knowledge,
countless the pious and their patrons,
countless warriors who face iron,
countless sages sunk in silent trance—
Who can express or fathom the creative power?

I cannot offer myself to you even once,
only that which pleases you is good.
You are forever constant, formless One.

18   Countless fools lost in pitch darkness,
countless thieves living off others,
countless tyrants bullying their way to immortality,
countless cut-throats with blood on their hands,
countless evil misdeeds trailing behind them,
countless liars spinning their lies,
countless perverts devouring filth,
countless slanderers bent by their burden.
Lowly Nanak thinks and says:
I cannot offer myself to you even once,
only that which pleases you is good.
You are forever constant, formless One.

19   Countless are your names, countless your places,
unreachable and unfathomable your countless spheres.
Even saying "countless" is a weight on our heads.
Yet by words we name, by words we acclaim,
by words we know and sing and praise.
By words we write, speak, and perform,
in words actions are written on our forehead,
        our blessed union proclaimed.[13]
Yet on the writer's forehead nothing is written,
as the One orders, so each of us receives.
As wide creation is, so is the name—
there is no place without it.

Who can express this creative power?
I cannot offer myself to you even once,
only that which pleases you is good.
You are forever constant, formless One.

Dirty hands feet skin body[14]   20
are washed clean with water.
Pee-stained clothes
are washed with soap too.
A mind polluted by evil
is cleansed by the color of the name.
Good and evil are not mere words,
the actions we do, get written and go with us:
we reap but what we sow,
Nanak: by the will we come and go.

Pilgrimage, austerity, mercy, gifts, charity—   21
their merit is barely worth a sesame seed.
By listening, embracing, and evoking love,
we scrub ourselves clean
     at the name's ford within.
Every virtue rests in you, in me I have none,
without doing good deeds devotion is impossible.
We praise you—our wealth, sacred verse, creator god,[15]
you are true, you are beauty, you are joy forever.
What was the time, the hour?
     What was the date, the day?
What was the season, the month,
     when creation took its form?

If pandits knew the time, it would be written in the
     Puranas,
if *qazis* knew the hour, it would be written in the Qur'an,
no yogi knows the date or day, no one knows the month or
     season,
only the creator knows who designed this creation.
How can I speak of the One?
     How can I praise?
     How can I describe?
     How can I know?
Nanak: how many speak of the One, each smarter than the
     other.
Great is the Sahib, great its name,
     all that happens is its doing.
Nanak: those who think they know
     are not adorned in the hereafter.

22   Worlds below worlds, million worlds above worlds.
     Tired of seeking their limits, the Vedas say it's all one
          thing,
     the Kateb say eighteen thousand,
          but really it is one reality.
     If it could be written it would have been written,
          but writing vanishes.
     Nanak: praise the great One
          who alone knows itself.

23   Praisers praise, but do not know your vastness
     like rivers and streams flow to the ocean
          unaware of its expanse.

Emperors and sultans rule over kingdoms vast as oceans,
    own wealth piled high as mountains,
yet none can match an ant whose mind does not forget.

Infinite is the One's glory and infinite the song of praise,   24
infinite the deeds and infinite the gifts,
infinite is the seeing, infinite the listening,
and infinite the workings of its mind.
Infinite are the created forms,
infinite the limits here and beyond.
How many cry, yearning to learn these limits?
Even their end is not to be found,
the end eludes us all,
the more it's expressed, the farther it extends.
Our Sahib is great, high its status,
and higher still its name.
Only were we ever to reach that height,
would we know the highest One.
Its greatness, it alone knows.
Nanak: the glance of love is its gift.

Great is your favor, how can one write about it?   25
Great the giver, with no trace of greed.
So many mighty heroes beg you
so many more than we can know.
So many waste themselves in vicious acts,
so many take and take yet deny their giver,
so many fools just eat and eat,
so many are devoured by pain and hunger, but
these too are your gifts, our giver.

Your will frees us from bondage,
no one else here has a say,
the fool who dares speak up
gets so many slaps on his face.
You alone know, you alone give,
how few though acknowledge this.
The person gifted to praise and adore,
Says Nanak, is truly the emperor of emperors.

26 Priceless are your virtues, priceless how they're traded,
priceless are their dealers, priceless the treasures in store,
priceless the customers, priceless what they take away,
priceless is love, priceless those immersed in it,
priceless is the law and priceless the court.
Priceless are the scales, priceless the weights,
priceless is bounty, priceless its sign,
priceless is the action, priceless the command.
How priceless the priceless One is, no one can say,
those who try are rapt in silence.
Vedas and Puranas say,
scholars say in their texts and discourses,
Brahmas say, Indras say,
gopīs and Govindas say,
Shivas say, siddhas say,
countless buddhas say,
demons say, gods say,
divine folks, silent sages, and the devout say.
How many speak and begin to speak,
how many have spoken and gone as they spoke.
Were their number doubled again,

14

no one still could say the slightest bit.
That One is as great as it chooses to be,
Nanak: only the true One knows itself.
The babbler who presumes to speak
is written down as the fool of fools.

What sort of gate is it, what house   27
    where you sit caring for all?[16]
So many instruments and melodies,
    so many musicians who praise you,
countless ragas and their fairies, we say,[17]
    and so many singers to sing to you.
To you sing wind, water, and fire,
    the king of righteousness sings at your door.[18]
To you sing Chitra and Gupta,[19]
    recording actions for the judge to decide.
To you sing Shiva, Brahma, and the goddess
    whose splendor you forever adorn.
To you sing Indras upon Indras[20]
    sitting among gods at the gate.
To you sing siddhas in meditation,
    to you sing sages in contemplation.
To you sing ascetics, the true, the contented,
    to you sing invincible heroes.
To you sing pandits and the best of seers
    reading the Vedas in every age.
To you sing beautiful women who enchant the mind
    in heaven, on earth, and in the netherworlds.
To you sing the jewels that you created
    along with the sixty-eight sacred sites.

15

To you sing heroes and mighty warriors,
    to you sing the four sources of life.[21]
To you sing continents, constellations, and universes—
    all created and sustained by you.
They sing to you, your devotees
    who please you and revel in your love.
How many others sing to you I can't imagine,
    Nanak, how can I think of them?
That One, the ever-true Sahib
    who is true, and whose name is true,
is and ever will be;
    never will the creator of the creation not be.
In many colors and many varied forms,
    the One who created illusion
watches everything it created.
    All this is the One's greatness.
Whatever the One desires comes to pass,
    no one can challenge its commands.
Nanak: all abide by the will
    of the emperor of emperors.

28   Contentment your yogic earrings, beauty your begging
    pouch,[22]
    smear yourself with the ashes of contemplation;
death shall be the cloak for your virgin body,
    and yoga and belief, the staff you lean on;
the Mother's sect accepts all people.[23]
    Conquer the mind to conquer the world.

All praise, all praise to the One—
timeless, pure, with no beginning or end,
    ever the same form, age to age.

With knowledge the banquet, and compassion the   29
    treasurer,[24]
    hear the sacred music sound in every heart.
The One is the master with all under its sway,
    why go for feats and miracles that lead you astray?
The One sets up our meeting, sets up our parting,
    we get what is written for us.
All praise, all praise to the One—
timeless, pure, with no beginning or end,
    ever the same form, age to age.

One mother, created in mystical union,   30
    three, her approved disciples:
creator, treasurer, and holder of court.
Everything works as the One decrees,
    all are under its command.
The One sees us all, yet marvel of marvels,
    none of us can see that One at all.
All praise, all praise to the One—
timeless, pure, with no beginning or end,
    ever the same form, age to age.

Its seat and its treasury are in every world.   31
Whatever is was placed there once for all time.
Ever creating, the creator beholds all it creates.

Nanak, the works of the true one are true forever.
All praise, all praise to the One—
timeless, pure, with no beginning no end,
    ever the same form, age to age.

32 If this one tongue became a hundred thousand,
        and each then became twenty times more,
    a hundred thousand times over they'd speak of
        the one name of Jagdish,* who owns the world.
    This is the way to climb the stairs to become one with the
        One.[25]
    Hearing these sky-high stories,
        even insects are spurred to imitate.
    Nanak: the One is attained by the gaze of love,
        not by the boasting of the false.

33 It's not for us to speak or stay silent,
    it's not for us to ask or give,
    it's not for us to live or die,
    it's not for us to gain riches that rattle the mind.
    It's not for us to have consciousness, knowledge, or
        reflection,
    it's not for us to escape the world-wheel,
    the One whose hand holds power watches over us all.
    Nanak: no one is too high or too low.

34 Nights and seasons, dates and days,
    air, water, fire, and netherworlds,

---

* "Master of the world," a term for the divine.

in their middle is the earth, the place of righteous action.
In its midst, lifestyles and beings of every hue,
with endless names and countless forms.
You reflect on every action,
you are true, truly just your court,
there the accepted five are adorned,[26]
their actions marked with the gaze of love.
The raw and the ripened are judged over there,[27]
Nanak: we come to know this when we reach.

Such is the order of the realm of duty,[28]   35
now tell us about the actions for the realm of knowledge.[29]
So many airs, waters, and fires,
    so many Krishnas and Shivas,
so many Brahmas fashioned in such variety of
    forms, colors, and guises.
So many earths and mountains to live and act in,
    so many Dhruvas to give instructions,[30]
so many Indras, moons, and suns,
    so many continents and universes,
so many siddhas, buddhas, naths,
    so many kinds of goddesses.
So many gods, demons, and sages,
    so many jewels and oceans,
so many species, so many languages,
    so many rulers and kings.
So many mystics, so many devotees,
    Nanak: there's just no end to their end.

36   In the realm of knowledge,
        knowledge blazes forth.
Here is numinous sound, feasting, cheering, and joy.
Now the realm of beauty is beauty itself,[31]
here shapes are inimitably designed.
Words fail description,
those who try, regret later.
Here consciousness, wisdom, mind, and discernment are
        sharpened,[32]
awareness whetted like the gods' and siddhas'.

37   The realm of action speaks of force.[33]
Here is the One, no other.
Here live heroes and mighty warriors,
filled with the strength of Ram.
Here are Sitas upon Sitas of great fame,[34]
their beauty beyond words.
They do not die, are not beguiled
for Ram is in their mind.
Here live devotees from many worlds
blissfully happy, for the true One beats in their heart.
In the realm of truth lives the formless One,[35]
ever creating,
        the One beholds with the gaze of blissful love.
Here are continents, constellations, universes
whose limits cannot be told.
Here are living beings of manifold forms,
all acting according to the will.
The One watches, rejoices, and reflects on its creation.
Nanak: to describe this is as hard as iron.

Discipline the smithy, patience the goldsmith,[36]   38
wisdom the anvil, knowledge the hammer,
with awe the bellows, stoke the fire within.[37]
Ambrosia pours out in the vat of love,[38]
the sacred word is cast in the true mint
—this is the action of those blessed by the gaze of love.
Nanak: those on whom the gaze falls are blissful and free.

Epilogue[39]
Air is our guru, water our father,
    the great earth our mother,
day and night, our female and male nurses
    in whose lap the whole world plays.
Good and bad, our actions are judged
    in the presence of righteousness,
it is they who take us near or far.
Those remembering the name,
    depart honored for their labor.
Nanak: their faces shine, and they carry with them
    many more to liberation.

EVENING HYMNS

That Gate

1

1 What sort of gate is that, what house[40]
      where you sit caring for all?[41]
So many your instruments and melodies,
      so many your musicians to praise you,
so many your ragas and their fairies,
      and so many singers to sing your song.
To you sing wind, water, and fire,
      the judge of righteousness sings at your door.
To you sing Chitra and Gupta,
      recording deeds for the judge to decide.
To you sing Shiva, Brahma, and the goddess
      whose splendor you forever adorn.
To you sing Indras upon Indras
      sitting among the gods at your gate.
To you sing siddhas in meditation,
      to you sing sages in contemplation.
To you sing ascetics, the true, the contented,
      to you sing invincible heroes.
To you sing pandits and the best of seers
      reading the Vedas in every age.
To you sing beautiful women who enchant the mind
      in heaven, on earth, and in the netherworlds.
To you sing the jewels that you created
      along with the sixty-eight sacred sites.

To you sing heroes and mighty warriors,
    to you sing the four sources of life.
To you sing continents, constellations, and universes—
    all created and sustained by you.
They sing to you, your devotees
    who please you, and revel in your love.
How many others sing to you I can't imagine,
    Nanak, how can I think of them?
That One, the ever-true Sahib
    who is true, and whose name is true,
is, and ever will be;
    never will the creator of creation not be.
In many colors and many varied forms,
    the One who created illusion
watches everything it created.
    All this is the One's greatness.
Whatever the One desires comes to pass,
    no one can challenge its commands.
Nanak: all abide by the will
    of the emperor of emperors.

2

We hear you are great,
    so we all say you are great.
We'd know your greatness
    if only we could see you.
We can't appraise you, we can't speak of you,
those who can, are rapt in you.

1

My great Sahiba, deep and unfathomable,
an ocean of virtues,
no one knows the extent of your dominion.

2 Mystics work and gather intuitions,
assessors work and gather calculations,
scholars, meditators, teachers, and their teachers,
none can estimate a grain of your greatness.

3 All truth, austerity, and all good deeds
all the powers of siddhas and others,
no one gains them without you.
With you we gain our actions, toll-free.[42]

4 How can our poor mouths speak
your praises, which burst forth from your treasury?
Those you give to, what do they lack?
Nanak: they are adorned by the true One.

3

1 If I say your name I live,
forget it, and I die.
To say the true name is so hard.
If I hunger for the true name
that hunger will devour my sorrow.

Mother, how could I forget
the true Sahib, whose name is true?

Many tried to say   2
    a grain of the true name's greatness
but failed to know its measure.
For all the praise we pour out,
the One is no more, no less.

That One never dies,   3
    we have no cause for mourning.
The One gives pleasures without end,
the virtue is this: there is no other,
never has been, nor will there ever be.

Great as you are, so too your gifts.   4
You created day for night to follow.
Those who forget you, husband,
    are the low caste,
Nanak: without the name,
    they're the lowest caste.

4

True guru, true Purakhu,   1
    we who love Hari pray to the guru.
Wretched worms, we seek shelter in the true guru,
    be kind and light us up with the name.

My friend Gurdev, light me up with Ram's name.
With every breath I take, my friend will be the name
    my guru taught me.
    Hari's praise will be my daily practice.[43]

2 How lucky are Hari's devotees,
      they thirst for Hari, soak in Hari's faith.
   Once they find the name, their thirst is quenched;
      once they meet true company, their virtues shine.

3 But those with no taste for Hari's name,
      unlucky ones, death catches them.
   They don't take shelter with the true guru, nor with true
      company:
      cursed in this life, cursed in the lives to come.

4 Those who seek shelter with the true guru,
      their foreheads glow, their luck was written when time
      began.
   Blessed, blessed good company, it brings taste for Hari's
      elixir,
      joining, Nanak lights up with the name.

5

1 My mind, why fret and fuss
      when precious Hari takes care of you?
   Were beings not created among rocks and mountains
      with food laid out before them?

   Descendant of Madhu, in true company, we become free.[44]
   Thanks to the guru, we reach the highest state,
      hearts dry as wood turn green.

2 Mothers, fathers, neighbors, sons, or wives,
      no one is support for another.

Our owner feeds each and every being,
  my mind, why fear?

She flies high, travels hundreds of miles   3
  leaving her young ones behind.
Who feeds them? Who teaches them to peck?
  My mind, have you ever considered this?

All the treasures and the eighteen powers   4
  sit in the palm of the master's hand.
Your devotee Nanak says, to you I offer myself again and
  again,
  I offer myself forever. Your limits have no end.

That Purakhu

1

Perfect is that Purakhu, Hari Purakhu is perfect.[45]   1
  Hari, beyond reach, grasp, or limit,
all meditate on you, my friend.[46]
  Hari, our true creator,
all beings belong to you, my friend
  you are their provider.
All saints contemplate you, my friend,
  Hari, you remove all suffering.
Hari is the master, Hari is the servant,
  Nanak: I am your lowly instrument.

2   You, the same Purakhu, are inside every being,
      my friend, Hari immersed in all.
Some are givers, some beggars, my friend,
      all part of your amazing play.
You give, you enjoy, my friend,
      I know no one but you.
You are the supreme being, with no end, my friend,
      which of your virtues can I describe?
To those who serve you, my friend,
      your slave Nanak offers himself.

3   Those who meditate on Hari, who meditate on you,
      my friend, live happily in this world.
Those who focus on Hari, my friend, are free,
      free, the noose of death lies slashed.
Those who focus on fearless Hari, my fearless friend,
      all their fears vanish.
Those who serve Hari, who serve my friend,
      take on Hari's own form.
Blessed, blessed are those who focus on Hari, my friend,
      says Nanak the slave, I offer myself to them.

4   Your devotion, your devotion is a treasury, my friend,
      it has no end, flows without end.
Your devotees, your devotees praise you, my friend,
      Hari, in many different ways with no end.
Multitudes worship you Hari, my friend,
      with no end of penance and meditation.
Multitudes read smritis and shastras, my friend,
      do the rituals and six actions to win you over.[47]

Worthy devotees are they, says Nanak your slave, worthy
    indeed, my friend,
        who please my Hari, the fortunate Bhagvanta.*

You, the Purakhu, are timeless and beyond creation, my   5
    friend,
        no one is as great as you.
You alone exist from age to age for ever and ever,
        the One, my friend, unchanging creator.
Whatever you will comes to be, my friend,
        whatever you do is done.
You birthed the entire creation, my friend,
        and you will take it all back.
Nanak, the slave, sings the creator's praise, my friend,
        who knows each and all.

2

You are my true creator, my beloved,
whatever pleases you will be,
    whatever is mine is what you give me.

Yours, all this is yours,   1
    it's you who is in everyone's mind.
Your compassion brings
    the jewel of the name.
Turn to the guru and get it,
    turn to yourself and lose it.

* "Fortune bestower," a term for the divine.

You drive us far from you,
    you bring us close too.
2 You are the ocean in which all live.
No other exists besides you,
    our life and living are your plaything.
Wrenched we join, joined we wrench apart,
    fortunately, you join us again.

3 Only those you teach, learn,
they speak and praise you no end.
They who serve Hari find happiness,
without effort, plunge into Hari's name.

4 You are the creator,
    all that gets done is by your doing.
No other is there besides you.
You create, behold, and know
    what you have done,
Says Nanak your slave,
    when we face the guru, it's you we see.

3

1 They live in this lake of fiery waters,
feet stuck in the slough of attachment,
    I see them sink.

My foolish mind, why not remember the One?
Leave Hari and your virtues rot away.
2 Neither ascetic nor true nor learned,[48]
    I am a fool, my life spins in craziness.

Nanak prays for the lap of refuge,
    with those who never forget you.

4

You've got this human body,   1
now is your chance to meet Gobind.
Nothing else will work
but to join the devout and recite the name.

Let's prepare to swim across the ocean,
life wanes in the dazzle of illusion.

I did no recitations or austerities,   2
    I was not disciplined or righteous,
I did not serve the devout nor recognize Hari the king,
Nanak: my actions are lowly,
I seek shelter in your lap, keep my honor.

LATE EVENING HYMN

Praise

1

1 If there is a home for praise and thoughts of our creator,[49]
let that home sing and remember.

Sing a wedding song to my fearless One,
I devote myself to a song bearing everlasting joy.

2 Day after day beings are nurtured
      Our giver looks after all.
Your gifts have no price,
      the giver is beyond account.

3 The wedding day is written, come friends,
      come pour the oil together.[50]
Give me your blessings, my friends,
      that I may join my Sahib.

4 Each home receives the marriage thread,[51]
      invitations are sent out to each and all.
Nanak: remember the sender,
      for the day will come for everyone.

2

1 Six schools with six leaders and six doctrines,[52]
but only one guru in countless forms.

Baba, the school that sings the song of our creator,[53]
make it your home. It will bring you honor.

Moments into seconds,　　　　　　　　　　　　　2
　　minutes into hours, days, dates, and months,
many seasons, but one sun.
Nanak: one creator with so many forms.[54]

3

The sky our platter, our lamps the sun and moon,　　1
　　pearls of starry galaxies shimmer around,
wafting sandal scents our incense, the breeze is our fly-
　　whisk,[55]
　　all vegetation our flower offerings to you.

What a worship.
Your worship breaks the cycle of birth and death,
the unstruck sound a silent kettledrum.

You have a thousand eyes. You have no eyes.　　　2
　　You have a thousand forms. You have no form.
You have a thousand pure feet. You have no feet.
　　You have no fragrance, yet your thousand fragrances
　　enchant me.

There is light in all, and that light is you,　　　　3
by that light we all are lit.
It shines with the guru's insight
whatever pleases you is your worship.

4   My mind, a greedy bumblebee,
      thirsts night and day for the elixir of Hari's lotus feet.
   Be kind, give this thirsty songbird a drink,
      Nanak longs to live in your name.

4

1   This body is a city teeming with lust and anger,[56]
      only true company shreds them to bits.
   Meeting the guru, written when time began,
      centers the mind in Hari's circle of circles.[57]

Join your palms to greet the devout,
     there's great merit in that.
Stretch yourselves out before them,
     there's great merit in that.

2   Self-seekers have no taste for Hari,[58]
      they are pierced by the thorns of I and Me.
   The more they move, the more piercing the pain,
      while the god of death stands with his staff ready.

3   Hari's devotees plunge in the name
      and out of the painful cycle of life and death.
   Paramesur, supreme, beyond destruction
      is theirs, and honor in worlds beyond worlds.

4   We may be poor and low, but we still belong to you Prabh,
      keep us with you Hari, highest of the high.

Nanak your slave says, your name alone is our support and
    shelter,
        our circle of bliss—Hari's name.

5

I beg you, listen to me, my friends,   1
    it's time to serve the saints.
Hari's profit earned here
    brings comfort in the hereafter.

Our life grows shorter by day and by night.
Join the guru, my mind, and all will be done.

This world is sunk in vices and doubts,   2
    those who know the ultimate being, swim across.
It wakes them up to taste the drink,
    they know the untold story.

Go for the deal you came for.   3
    Join the guru, lodge Hari in your mind,
and serenely enjoy the palace in your home,
    the circle of birth and death will be no more.

Knower of hearts, Purakhu, maker,   4
    you fulfill our deepest desires,
Your slave Nanak asks, give me this joy,
    make me the dust of the saint's feet.[59]

Ballad in the
Melody of Hope

Ballad with lyrics, also by the first Guru, in the melody of
the maimed King As.[1]

1

A hundred times a day, I circle my guru   M1
who turns humans into gods without delay.

If a hundred moons shine out and a thousand suns blaze   M2
    forth,
without the guru,
    such dazzling brilliance is still pitch dark.

Nanak: oblivious of the guru, they think they are wise;   M1
they lie lifeless in the field, tossed away as useless weed.
Thrown out in the field, says Nanak, they must please a
    hundred masters.
They are stuffed with ash, wretched things, decked in
    fruits and flowers.

Envoi[2]
You designed yourself, named yourself,
next you laid out this creation, now
    sit watching in joyous wonder.
You are the giver and the creator,
    how you rejoice making your expanse.
Knower of all, you give and take life with a single call.
Sit watching in joyous wonder.

2

M1 True are your realms, true the constellations,
   true your worlds and true the shapes,
   true your actions and all your thoughts,
   true your order, true your court,
   true your will, true your verdict,
   true your grace and your sign.[3]
   Millions upon millions call you true,
   all your power is true, and so is your force.
   Your praise is true, and true your song,
   your nature is true, our true emperor.[4]
   Nanak: true ones focus on truth,
   liars go from birth to birth.

M1 Great is your praise, for your name is great,
   great is your praise, for your justice is true,
   your praise is great, for your seat is steady,
   your praise is great, for you know all we say,
   your praise is great, for you recognize all love,
   your praise is great, for you give before we ask,
   your praise is great, for everything is you.
   Nanak: we can't tell any of your doings,
   All that is done, all to be done
         is your will alone.

M2 This world is a cabin for the true One to live in.
   By its order some merge with it, others are cast aside.
   Its will lifts some up, others remain deluded.
   No one can guess whom the One blesses,

Nanak: the guru-centered know,
    the One enlightens them.

Envoi
Nanak: you gave birth to beings
    wrote your name and enthroned morality.[5]
Truth and truth alone decides in the hereafter,
    the foul are picked out and cast aside.
Liars find no place,
    black-faced, they're sent to hell.
Winners are dyed in your name,
    deceivers, defeated.
You wrote your name and enthroned morality.

3

Wondrous the numinous sound, wondrous the Vedas,   M1
wondrous are beings, wondrous their diversity,
wondrous the forms, wondrous all the hues,
wondrous the people who go about nude,
wondrous is air, wondrous is water,
wondrous is fire playing wonders,
wondrous this earth, wondrous its species,
wondrous the tastes bewitching us beings,
wondrous is union, wondrous is parting,
wondrous is hunger, wondrous its contentment,
wondrous is praise, wondrous the song,
wondrous going astray, wondrous walking the path,
wondrous is intimacy, wondrous being apart,
wondrous to see the ever-present One.

Seeing these wonders, I'm wonderstruck.
Nanak: the perfectly blessed perceive them.

M1   In your creation we see you, we hear you in your creation,[6]
     in your creation lie our joys and fears.
Your creation are the skies, the nether regions,
     your creation, all the visible forms,
your creation the Vedas, the Puranas, the Kateb,
     your creation is all thinking,
your creation our eating, drinking, dressing up,
     your creation all the love within us,
your creation the species so diverse and colorful,
     your creation all the beings of the world,
your creation is virtue, your creation is vice,
     your creation is our honor and pride,
your creation is air, water, fire,
     your creation, earth and dust,
all is your creation, you are our mighty creator,
     and your name is the purest of the pure.
Nanak: all is seen and given by your will,
     You are matchless.

Envoi
You make bumblebees dance in pleasure,
     then turn them to ashes and blow them away.
People may be wealthy and worldly,
     still they'll be dragged out
     with chains around their necks.
Deeds of praise are read out in the hereafter,
     misdeeds in the record are explained.

They receive no shelter, they're beaten up,
   their cries go unheard,
the ignorant blind lose out on life.

4

In fear the breeze blows forever,   M1
in fear flow millions of rivers,
in fear fire flares up to perform forced labor,
in fear earth bears its burden.
In fear Indra walks around upside down,
in fear the king of righteousness stands at his door.
In fear is the sun, in fear the moon,
go a million miles with no end.
In fear live siddhas, Buddhas, gods, and naths
In fear the skies stretch across
In fear live warriors brave and strong
In fear shiploads come and go
The writing of fear is written over everyone,
Nanak: only the formless truth is fearless.

Nanak: fearless and formless is the one alone.   M1
   How many Rams of dust blow around
   How many Krishna tales abound
   How many thoughts on the Vedas
   How many dancing beggars
   tumble and spin in perfect tempo?
Magicians come to the bazaar,
   concocting their own shows.
Kings and queens sing,
   blabber all sorts of things,

their earrings cost thousands,
 their necklaces even more,
the body that wears them, Nanak,
 turns to dust.
Knowledge is not found in words,
 to explain this is hard as iron.[7]
Good actions earn us success,
 being clever or giving orders is useless.

Envoi
If you give us your gaze of love,
 we get to see the true guru.
This life cycles birth after birth
 till we hear the true guru's word.
No giver is as great as the true guru,
 people, listen.
Get rid of your selfish self,
 meet the true guru and find truth.
He reveals the truth of truths.

5

M1 The twenty-four hours are milkmaids,
 the quarters of the day, Krishna the cowherd,
the jewels are air, water, and fire,
 sun and moon, their incarnations.
All the wealth and fortunes of this earth
 trap us in their dealings.
Nanak: the ignorant are looted,
 death's messenger devours them.

Disciples play music, teachers dance,   M1
kick their feet, toss their heads around,
dust flies off, gets in their hair,
people watch, laugh, and return home.
A rhythmic beat for a piece of bread,
they dash themselves onto the ground,
they sing of milkmaids, sing of Krishna,
sing of Sita and kings like Ram.
The true name, free of fear or enmity,
choreographs the whole cosmos.
Servants who serve with pleasing acts,
delicious are their nights, for they're in love.
Seekers train their mind on the guru
who sees their actions by the gaze of love,
        carries them across.
Oil press, spinning wheel, grinding stone, potter's wheel,
countless whirlwinds in the desert,
spinning tops, churning rods, threshers,
birds spiraling breathlessly on and on,
living beings spinning on a spike,
Nanak, no count or end to this whirling.
The One who binds all in bondage, spins us around.
We each dance in step with our actions.
They who laugh as they dance, weep when they leave,
they don't fly high nor gain *siddhi* powers,
they jump up and down to amuse themselves.
Nanak, those in awe of you,
        love you.[8]

45

Envoi
Your name is the formless One,
    we call on and escape hell.
Our body and breath belong to you,
    why beg you for food?
Want something good?
    Do good, live low.
Try as we may to elude the tyranny of death,
    it creeps on us in some way,
nobody lingers once their time is up.

6

M1   Muslims praise the Sharia,
      read and mull it over and over,
your slaves enslave themselves to behold you.[9]
Hindus exalt the exalted, visualize the infinite form,
bathe at sacred sites, worship their gods
    with fragrant sandal incense.
Yogis meditate in the void on the names of the unseen
    creator,
visualize the subtle pure name in their body's shape.
The virtuous are content figuring how to give,[10]
they give and give but ask the world to honor them
    a thousand times.
Useless thieves, adulterers, liars, villains
consume this world's good, and depart—
    what good have they done?
On water and land, across worlds and spheres,
    beings upon beings in form upon form,

you know all they say, but
    they too have a sense of your reality.[11]
Nanak: your devotees hunger to praise
    your true name, their life food,
they live in bliss day and night,
    even their feet's dust is good.[12]

The clay from a Muslim's grave   M1
    ends in the potter's wheel,
molded into jars and brick,
    heated in the furnace, it cries out,[13]
louder and louder the poor clay wails
    as crackling sparks lash out more and more.
Nanak: the creator who creates,
    alone knows what it does.

Envoi
Without the true guru no one can know the One,
    without the true guru no one has ever known it.
The One became one with the true guru
    to reveal its words for us to hear.[14]
Those who let their cravings go,
    find the true guru and are free forever.
It's best to think of the true One,
this is how we find our giver,
    the life of the universe, Jagjivan.

7

Saying I we come, saying I we go,   M1
saying I we are born, saying I we die,

saying I we give, saying I we take,
saying I we gain, saying I we lose,
saying I we are true or fake,
saying I we reflect on good and bad,
saying I we appear in heaven or hell,
saying I we laugh, saying I we cry,
saying I we fall in dirt, saying I we clean up,
saying I we lose caste and class,
saying I we are stupid, saying I, wise,
we don't see the value of freedom or liberation.
Saying I is illusion, saying I, shadows,
doing I-me deeds we beings come to be,
discern the I-me, see the divine gate,
without insight we argue and fight.
Nanak: by the will our account is written,
as we are seen, so we see.

M2 It's the nature of I-me
        to lead us to selfish acts
    the trap of I-me
        brings us birth over and again.
    Where does I-me come from?
        How do we let it go?
    I-me comes from the will,
        we act by what we did before.
    I-me is a chronic sickness,
        yet also holds its cure.[15]
    If the One is kind to us,
        we live by the guru's holy word.

Says Nanak, listen my people, for
    this is how pain goes away.

Envoi
Those who serve you are serene,
    they focus on truth, truth alone.
They do not step on muck,
    earn merit by their good actions,
break free of worldly fetters,
    eat and drink in moderation.
You are the foremost giver,
    each day you give us more and more.
We praise greatness, we find the great One.

8

People, trees, fords, riverbanks, clouds, fields,   M1
islands, continents, constellations, planets, universes,
egg, womb, earth, and sweat born,
oceans, mountains, beings, Nanak,
    only the One knows the limits.
Nanak: the One births beings and treasures each one,
the creator who creates also cares for us,
the creator who creates this world,
    worries about it.
I greet and bow to the One,
    praise its everlasting court.
Nanak: without the true name,
    what's a holy dot? A sacred thread?

M1   We may act nobly a thousand times,
        be generous a thousand times over,
perform untold penance at sacred sites,
        practice the yoga of serenity in deserted places.[16]
We may win countless brave battles,
        even die on the battlefield.
Read and recite a thousand shrutis and Puranas,
        study a thousand forms of knowledge and thought.
The creator who sets us off on our doings,
        also wrote down our coming and going.
Nanak: thoughts are just an illusion,
        our actions must have the sign of truth.

Envoi
You are the One true Sahib,
        you spread truth, truth alone.
Those you give to,
        hold on to truth, live in truth.
They found truth by joining the guru,
        truth flows in their heart.
Fools don't know what truth is,
        self-centered, lose out on life.
Why, why did they even enter this world?

9

M1   We may read cartloads of books,
        caravans of books,
we may read boatloads of books,
        fill caverns with the books we've read,

we may read year after year,
    month by month,
we may read through our entire life,
    read with each breath we take.
Nanak: one item alone gets recorded,
    the rest is pompous froth.

The more we write and read,   M1
the more we are frustrated.
The more we go on pilgrimages,
the more we boast.
The more guises we take,
    the more our body hurts.
My life, you reap what you sow.
Giving up food, we lose our sense of taste.
In love with duality, we suffer terribly.
Living nude,
groaning day and night,
keeping silent,
    we damage ourselves.
Without the guru, how to wake from sleep?
Those who go barefoot,
suffer their own doing,
eat crumbs and leftovers,
    smear their head with ashes,
dimwits with no dignity.
Except the name, nothing avails.
They live in jungles, cemeteries, graveyards,
blind idiots who grieve at the end

but those who meet the true guru, rejoice,
their minds embrace Hari's name.
Nanak: in the gaze of love they see you,
live free of hope and anxiety,
 the sacred word burns off their I-me.

Envoi
Your devotees entice you, they look so lovely,
 sing your song at your door.
Nanak: those bereft of good actions
 are lost, without support.
Clueless of their very source,
 they pump up their hollow self.
They can call themselves great all they want,
 I am a songster, a low-caste songster,[17]
let me be among those who sing your praise.

10

M1 False is the king, false his subjects,
 false this whole world.
False are pavilions, false the mansions,
 false all who live in them.
False is gold, false is silver,
 false all who wear them.
False this body, false its clothing,
 false is infinite beauty.
False the husband, false the wife,
 they all soon turn to dust.
The false fall for the false,
 forget the creator.

Who are my friends?
>The whole world is in flux.
False are sweets, false is honey,
>falling for falsehood, boatloads drown.
Nanak humbly says,
>without you all is utterly false.

We get to know truth   M1
>when we polish our hearts to be true,
false filth washes off,
>our body gets clean and fresh.
We get to know truth
>when we fall in love with it,
our mind revels in the sound of the name,
>freedom's door opens wide.
We get to know truth
>when we learn to live,
we cultivate our body,
>sow it with the creator's seed.
We get to know truth
>when we attain true teaching,
nurture empathy for fellow beings,
>hand out alms, do pious deeds.
We get to know truth
>when we reside in the sacred site deep in us,
sit still and ask the true guru,
>abide by the response.
Truth is the only cure for all,
>washing away the false.
Nanak seeks truth from those who hold it in their scarf.[18]

Envoi
The gift I seek is the dust off their feet,
    I'll smear it on my forehead if I get it.
Give up lies and greed,
    single-mindedly, think of the One unseen.
We gather the fruit of what we do,
we may get dust if that's what was written,[19]
by narrow-minded service, we lose it all.

11

M1 A famine of truth, lies prevail,
    it's all ghosts in this dark time.
Those who sowed the seed, depart in honor.
    Does split seed ever sprout?
A whole seed grows, if it's the season.
Nanak: raw fabric absorbs color
    only when steeped in alum.[20]
Pour divine awe in the dyeing vat[21]
    to dye this body in beauty.
Nanak: a body dyed in devotion
    is free of the faintest stain.

M1 Greed and evil are king and minister:
    they appoint falsity as treasurer,
consult with lust, their adviser.
    Together, they sit and think
while their subjects, blind and ignorant,
    obey them, corpselike.

The wise dance, play music,
    dress themselves up in finery,
cheer out loud as they sing of battles and heroes' songs.
A foolish pandit loves to raise clever arguments.
The righteous lose their righteousness,
    when they ask for the door of liberation.
So-called ascetics who leave home and society
    don't know the way.
We all call ourselves perfect,
    nobody says any less;
Nanak: when our weight of honor is weighed in the
    hereafter,
    then we shall truly know our weight.

What we do shows up,   M1
    Nanak: the true One sees it all.
Everybody jumps up to act on their own,
    only what the creator does is done.
Caste has no power in the hereafter,
    out there, it's a whole new life.
Those whose honor is recorded,
    they alone are good.

Envoi
Those set to do good at the beginning of time,
    they remember you, husband.
You created this variegated world,
    we creatures have no control.

Some you join with yourself,
  some you lead astray.
With the guru's kindness we find
  the place you reveal yourself.
Serenely we plunge into truth.

12

M1 Pain is medicine, pleasure disease,
   since where there's pleasure, there's no you.
  It's you who do, creator, I am nothing;
   anything I do, fails.

I rejoice in the creation you live in,
yet I cannot see your limits.

M1 Your light is in our birth,[22]
   we are known in your light.
   Your artless art is all over.
  You are the true Sahib,
   glorious is your praise,
   those who praise you swim across.
  Nanak: let us speak of our creator,
   who does all that is to be done.

M2 For yogis, the sacred word is knowledge,
   for Brahmans, it is the Vedas,
  heroism for Kshatriyas,
   for Shudras, serving others.
  The sacred word of words is the One
   —those who know the secret

are no different from the stainless god,
    Nanak is their slave.

The one Krishna is the god of all gods,   M2
    the god of our very self as well.[23]
To those who discover the secret,
    Vasudeva is their very self.
They're no different from the stainless god,
    Nanak is their slave.

A pitcher always carries water,   M1
    without it, it's no pitcher.
Our mind contains knowledge,
    without the guru,
    it has no knowledge there.

Envoi
When a scholar errs, punish him,
    not an illiterate saint.
We should be named for the actions we do,
don't play games that fail in the divine court.
The learned and the ignorant
    will be reckoned in the hereafter,
the self-willed are beaten over there.

13

A chariot and charioteer   M1
    make up the peak body, Nanak.[24]
From age to age they change,
    so the wise realize.[25]

In the golden age, righteousness, the charioteer,
  drove the chariot of contentment.
In the silver age,
    strength
      drove the chariot of asceticism.
In the bronze age,
    truth
      drove the chariot of penance.
In this dark age,
    lies
      drive the fiery chariot of lust.

M1 *Sama Veda* says the guide is white-clad.[26]
      In the age of truth, we lived in truth,
        everybody was plunged in truth.
    Ṛg Veda says the one flows all over,
        Ram's name glows, a sun among the gods.
        Take up the name so that vices leave,
          find freedom deep within, says Nanak.
    In *Yajur Veda,* Chandravali was forcefully seduced[27]
        by Kanhu Krishna the Yadav,
        he brought the coral tree for his milk girl,[28]
        and reveled in Vrindavan.
    In this dark age *Atharva Veda* prevails,
        Allah has become the name of god;
    donning royal blue robes,
        Turks and Pathans rule.[29]
    The four Vedas are true for those

who read, recite, reflect on them
　　in each of the four ages.
And with love and devotion,
　　living low,
Nanak: we find freedom within.

Envoi
I circle the true guru
　　who made me treasure our husband.
He taught me to line my eyes with knowledge,
　　now they see the whole universe.
Those who trade in their husband for another,
　　drown in ignorance.
The true guru is the ship,
he ferries graciously across the few who dwell on it.

14

The silk-cotton tree, tall and dense,　　　　M1
　　shoots to the skies like an arrow.
Birds fly over in hope,
　　only to fly away in despair.
Its fruit is bland, its flowers repugnant,
　　its leaves good for nothing.
Nanak: sweet humility is the virtue of virtues.
We all bow to ourselves and no one else,
the wider side dips lower on a scale.
The corrupt stoop twice as low,
　　hunters stoop over deer tracks.

Why bother bending your head
if your heart heads in the wrong direction?

M1 They read scriptures, say evening prayers, debate,
worship images and, storklike, meditate.
Lies are on their lips, yet they put on jewels,
thrice a day they contemplate the three-line hymn.[30]
They wear a rosary around the neck,
a holy mark on the forehead,
a twice-folded cloth around the waist,
a cover over their head.
If only they knew what the ultimate being does,
they'd see how futile their acts are.
Nanak says, focus with resolve,
without the true guru, we run off course.

Envoi
Clothing and beautiful things
are all left behind in this world.
We reap good or bad
for each action we do.
Here we dictate to our heart's content
there we'll walk the narrow lane.
Naked we'll be steered to scary hell.
We'll regret each wrong we did.

15

M1 The cotton of compassion, spun in contentment,
knotted in self-discipline with a twist of truth

is a holy thread.
    Pandit, invest me with this thread of life,
which neither snaps nor soils,
    never burns nor gets lost.[31]
Nanak: blessed are the people
    who wear it round their neck as they go about.
But with four cowries' worth of thread,
    seated on the square platform,
the Brahman priest whispers teachings in the ear,
    a guru now.
At death this thread falls off,
    he departs without it.

Untold thefts, untold adulteries,   M1
    untold lies, untold abuses,
untold tricks and secrets are met out night and day.
Yet the sacred thread is put on, cotton spun
    brought and twisted by the Brahman priest,
a goat is slaughtered, cooked, feasted on;
    everybody ordains that it be worn.[32]
When the thread frays it is tossed,
    a new one worn;
Nanak: the thread would not break, were it strong.

To win respect, embrace the name,   M1
    praise truth as ritual thread,
go to its court wearing it, my sons,
    such a thread never frays.

M1   There is no thread for the senses,
       no thread for women.
Daily at dawn his beard is spat upon.[33]
No thread for the feet, no thread for the hands,
no thread for the tongue, no thread for the eyes.
Without thread, he goes about[34]
yet twists threads for others,
charges couples for weddings,
reads horoscopes to teach the way.
My people, come hear of this miracle
—the ignorant is called wise.[35]

Envoi
If kind Sahib is kind to us,
      we do what he says.
Servants serve him as they should,
      if he makes them embrace his will.
Embrace his will, and be greeted
      in the husband's palace.
When we do as he desires,
      our desires come true.
We enter divine court in glorious robes.

16

M1   You tax cows and Brahmans, yet
      expect cow-dung plaster to release you?[36]
You wear loincloth, a holy dot, carry a rosary,
      then eat the foreigners' food?[37]

At home you do *puja,* you read Muslim texts in public,
    why act as Turks, brothers?[38]
Get rid of such pretense,
swim across,
    grasp the name.

Those feed on humans, yet say *namaz.*   M1
These wear the sacred thread, yet wield the knife;
Brahman sounds echo in their home,
yet they relish the same food.
Their stock is scam, business is scam,
they earn their livelihood spreading scams.
Beauty and morality stay afar,
Nanak: stuffed as they are with lies.
With a holy dot on their forehead,
    loincloth folded round their waist,
knives in hand to butcher the world,
they don blue outfits to win the rulers,
seek donations from the foreigners,
    but worship their Puranas,
eat forbidden goat others slaughtered,
yet forbid others to enter their kitchen square.
Four lines mark the sacred space
where these liars come and sit.
"Don't touch, don't touch," they say,
"you'll pollute our food."
Their defiled bodies do evil deeds,
with dirty minds they rinse their mouths.

Nanak: let's focus on truth,
live purely, attain the true One.

Envoi
We're all in your consciousness,
 your gaze of love animates us.
You give us praise, make us work,
the greatest of the great on this great earth,
 you assign to each their task.
But if you avert your gaze of love,
 mighty sultans turn to blades of grass,
beg at doors and get no scrap.

17

M1 Robbers break into houses,
  for oblations to their ancestors.
Their stolen goods are seized ahead,[39]
  their ancestors branded as robbers, too.
When justice is meted out,
  the hands of middlemen are cut off.
Nanak: only offerings from honest work
  are rewarded in the hereafter.

M1 As a woman's period flows month after month,[40]
lies on a liar's lips spill day after day.
Don't call pure those who sit with bathed bodies,
Nanak: they are pure who enshrine
  in their minds
   the One.

Envoi
Saddled horses fast as wind,
    harems decked in every hue,
they lie sprawled
    in towering mansions and palaces,
doing as they please, yet fail
    to recognize Hari.
Indulging in their orders, gloating over their mansions,
    they forget death,
Old age sneaks up, youth is lost.

18

If we follow the code of pollution,   M1
    pollution is all over.
Maggots breed in cow dung and firewood,
life breeds in every food grain.
First, water is life itself,
    nothing sprouts without it.
How can we believe in pollution
    when it's all over our kitchen?
Nanak: there's no way to escape pollution,
    true knowledge alone washes it off.

The mind's pollution is greed,   M1
    the tongue's is lies.
The pollution of the eyes,
    to covet another's wife, wealth, beauty.
The ears' pollution is to hear malice
    and thrive on mistrust.

Nanak: this way a swanlike human flies
    bound for the city of death.

M1   All pollution is mere doubt,
    attachment to duality.
Birth and death are divine command,
    by the will, we come and go.
All our eating and drinking are pure,
    gifts from the One to nourish us.
Nanak: the guru-centered perceive,
    nothing is polluted for them.

Envoi

Praise the greatness of the true guru,
    spring of the greatest virtues.
We see them if our husband joins us,
    they lodge in us if he's pleased.
With his hand on our forehead,
    his will expels the wrongs in us.
Once the husband delights in us,
    all nine treasures are ours.[41]

19

M1   First, the priest purifies himself,[42]
    then sits in a pure spot,
dishes yet to be tasted or served
    are placed before him.
He eats pure food and gets purer still,
    he begins reading his sacred verse

his purities turn to waste—
    now who's to be blamed?
Grain is divine, water is divine, fire is divine,
    salt too, and by adding ghee, the fifth,
our food becomes more divine.
But touched by an evil person,
    it turns so filthy it's spat out.
A mouth that eats tasty food and sings
    without the name,
Nanak: think of it as spat upon.

Of woman we are born, in woman conceived,   M1
    to a woman engaged and married.
Through woman we gain companionship,
    through woman the course of life moves on.
Upon a woman's death, another one is sought,
    by woman bonds are established.
Why then call her polluted?
    Who gives birth to kings?[43]
From woman, woman is born,
    from woman all are bodied forth.
Nanak: the only exception is the true One.
The mouths that sing its praise
    are blessed four times over,
Nanak: their faces glow in its true court.

Envoi
All say, "this is mine,"
    those who don't are singled out.

We each must settle the account of our own actions.
We are not in this world to stay,
    why let pride wear us down?
"Don't call anyone bad,"
    read these words, act upon them,
don't squabble with fools.

20

M1   Nanak, if what we say is dull,
    body and mind turn dull too.
We are called the dullards of the dull,
    we have no taste at all.
Dullards get thrown out of the court,
    dull faces are spat upon.
Dullards are called fools,
    thrashed with shoes as punishment.

M1   Fake within, honored without,
    you find these types the world over.
They bathe at sixty-eight sacred sites,
    yet dirt clings to them.
In this world the best wear rags,
    but are silken within.
Gaze transfixed with love for Rabb
blushing at him
    whether they laugh or cry or hold their silence,
they care for nothing except true love.
They wait begging at his threshold,
    eat only when he gives.

There is one court, one pen,
    there you and I will meet
to face our record. Nanak:
    offenders will be crushed like oilseeds.

Envoi
You made your creation,
    filled it with your art.
You watch your own doing,
    hold both your raw and ripened beings.[44]
All who have come, must go,
    each in their turn.
Why forget the Sahib
    who owns life and breath?
Actions lie in our hands,
    let's try to do better.

21

What kind of a love affair is it   M2
    if one's attracted to another?
Nanak: lovers are constantly rapt in their love.
Those who do good in return for good,
    or bad in return for bad,
aren't fit to be called lovers;
    they're mere record keepers.

First they gush, then answer back—   M2
    they went astray right from the start.
Nanak: insincere in both their acts,
    they find no refuge.

Envoi

Always treasure the Sahib
    whose service earns happiness.
We reap what we sow, so why act immorally?
Do no evil, keep an eye on the future,
make sure we roll the dice
    so not to lose out to the Sahib.
Do actions that build up profit.

22

M2 Proud and hostile servants are losers,
who prattle on and never please their master.
The honorable give themselves up in service,
Nanak: enticed, they entice the One,
    their union succeeds.

M2 What lies deep inside blossoms forth,
    what slips from the lips is wind.
We sow poison and ask for elixir?
    What justice is this?

M2 Friendship with fools bears no fruit,
it's so obvious they act by the little they know.
One thing merges into another if no distance is in
    between.
No order makes it through to the Sahib,
    make intimate requests.
Nanak: by wrongdoing we ruin ourselves,
    singing divine praise, we blossom.

Friendship with an idiot, love for a big shot, M2
are like lines on water—
    no place, no trace.

In idiots' hands tasks fail invariably, M2
they may get one or two right,
    the rest will go wrong.

Envoi
Serve as servants, follow the master's wish,
your honor will grow, your salary will double.
Going against the master will earn you shame,
no salary, a good shoe thrashing on your face.
Praise to the One whose gifts we eat,
Nanak: no order makes it through to the master,
    only intimate requests.

23

Is it a gift if we ask for it? M2
Nanak: miraculous is the gift
    given by Sahib for pleasure.

Is it service if done in fear of the master? M2
Nanak: spot the servant who serves
    merged in the master.

Envoi
Nanak: Hari's ends or limits can't be seen.
The One gives birth to creation, destroys it as well.

Some are chained by the neck,
    others gallop away with riches.
The One is the doer, also makes us do,
    to whom else can we cry?
Nanak: the One who made this creation,
    cares for it as well.

24

M1 The One shapes all clay jars, fills them too.
Some turn into milk pots, others into ash.
Some slide into blankets to sleep,
    others must stand guard.
Nanak: they are perfected
    who receive its gaze of love.

M2 The One shapes and creates, maintains us all,
watches its creation take shape and vanish.
Nanak: whom should we call out to?
    Everything is the One, nothing else.

Envoi
The greatness of the great One
    no telling can tell.
Mighty and merciful, our creator
    gives all beings their bread,
when time began,
    assigned us our actions.
Nanak: besides the One there is no refuge.
The One does only as the One wants to. *(Corrected.)*[45]

Discourse with the Siddhas

A gathering of siddhas sit in yogic pose.[1]
   "Greetings to this pious gathering.
Before the true One, infinite and unfathomable,
I place my severed head,
   I give my body and mind.
Says Nanak,
   we find truth in the company of saints,
   effortlessly we win loving praise.

Why wander far? Truth is living purely.
Without the true sacred word there's no release."

"Who are you? What's your name?
   What's your path? What's your aim?"
"I speak truly, I beg you, I offer myself to saints."[2]
"Where is your seat? Young man, where do you live?
   Where do you come from, where are you headed?
Tell Nanak,
   let the detached hear of your way."

"Live with the One who sits in every heart,
   walk the way dear to the true guru.
Freely we come and go by the will,
   Nanak, we abide by it forever.
The guru taught me to sit like the still Narayana.[3]
Those facing the guru realize their very self,
   the true ones merge with truth."

"This world-ocean is dangerous, they say,
   how do we cross it?" Charpat asks,[4]

1

2

3

4

"Nanak, you shook off the world,
    give me your true perspective."
"If one who asks already knows,
    what answer can you give?
Surely, if you've already crossed,
    what position can I offer?

5   Freely, a lotus floats in water,
        a duck paddles in a pond;
    when consciousness swims in the sacred word,
        Nanak: we cross the world-ocean,
        saying the name.
    Set apart, alone, focused on the One,
        living amid desires without desire,
    when such a person sees the One,
        unfathomable, imperceptible,
        and shows others,
        Nanak is their slave."

6   "Guide, hear our request,
        we want your true response.
    Don't be mad, tell us
        how do we reach the guru's door?"
    "Nanak: this racing mind
        once resting in the name
        settles into its true home.
    We fall in love with truth, the creator
        joins us in union."

7   "Away from shops and busy roads,
        amid forest trees and plants

surviving on fruits and roots:
    this is the knowledge renunciates give.
Bathing at pilgrimage fords
    reaps fruits of happiness, unspoiled by pollution.
Gorakh's disciple Loharipa says,
    this is the path of yoga."

"Don't fall asleep in shops or roads,   8
    don't let consciousness wander
    into the house of others.
Nanak: without the name,
    no mind is balanced, no hunger slaked.
Shops and cities within my own house
    the guru showed me,
    where true business goes on in peace.
Sleep less, eat little, says Nanak,
    this is the essence of knowledge.

Make divine vision your attire, king of yogis,   9
    your earrings, pouch, and patched cloak.[5]
Serve the One within as your twelve branches of yoga,
    let the single path be your six schools of philosophy.[6]
Instruct the mind this way, my friend,
    and we will be hurt no more.
Those centered on the guru get it, says Nanak,
    this is the way to master yoga.

Our earrings, the sacred word forever within us,[7]   10
    rid us of ego and attachment.

Realizing the guru's sacred word
    destroys lust, anger, and arrogance.
Our cloak and pouch are the all-pervasive One,
    Hari alone takes us across, Nanak.
From the guru's pure speech we discern,
    true is the Sahib, true its name.

11   Their mind turned over as begging bowl,
        the five elements woven into a cap,[8]
their body a meditation mat,
    their mind a loincloth,
with truth, contentment, discipline as companions,
those who face the guru treasure the name, Nanak says."

12   "Who is hidden? Who is free?
Who joins the within with the without?
Who comes, who goes?
Who permeates the three worlds?"

13   "Hidden in every heart is the One.
    Those who face the guru are free.
Within and without are joined by the sacred word.
Those faced toward the self
    are lost in cycles of coming and going,
Nanak:
    those who face the guru,
    merge with truth."

14   "How are we bound? Devoured by the serpent?[9]
How do we lose and win?

How do we become pure or get lost in darkness?
Anyone who reflects on this reality
   will be our guru."

"Ignorance binds us, illusion's serpent devours us.   15
Centered on the ego we lose, on the guru we win.
We meet the true guru, darkness disappears,
Nanak: I-me goes,
   we are merged.

Bound to the absolute void within,[10]   16
the swan won't escape,
   the frame won't break.
In the serene cave of the heart truth appears,
Nanak: true ones are loved by truth."

"Wandering ascetic, why did you leave home?[11]   17
Why did you take this form?
What stock do you trade in?
How will you carry others across?"

"I became a wandering ascetic
   to find those who face the guru;
I took this form to meet them.
Truth is the stock I trade in.
Nanak: those facing the guru go across."   18

"Young man, how did you change your course of birth?   19
What did you set your mind on?
How did you end hopes and expectations?

How did you find the unmediated light?
Without teeth, how do you eat iron?
Nanak, give us your true perspective."

20   "Birth in the true guru's house ended my rounds,[12]
my mind tuned to the unstruck sound.[13]
The sacred word burnt hopes and expectations,
facing the guru, I saw the unmediated light.
Once the three strands are gone, you can chew iron,[14]
Nanak: the swimmer helps one swim across."

21   "What are your thoughts on the very beginning?
           Where was void housed then?
What do you say about knowledge's earrings?
           Who resides in every heart?
How do we burn the mace of death?
           How do we enter the fearless state?
How do we learn the pose of serene contentment?
           How to destroy our enemies?"
"When the guru's sacred word kills toxic I-me,
           we begin living in our home within.
Whoever recognizes the sacred word
           of the creator of creation,
           Nanak is his slave."

22   "Where do we come from? Where do we go?
           Where do we stay absorbed?
One who clarifies the sacred word,
           is a guru without a grain of greed.

How do we find the reality of the imperceptible?
    How do the guru-facing fall in love?
He is all-consciousness, he is the creator;
    give us your thoughts, Nanak."
"By the will we come, by the will we go,
    in the will we stay absorbed.
We live truth through the perfect guru,
    we trace its limitless limits through the sacred word.

Imagine the beginning as absolute wonder,   23
    unmediated void existed, we say.
To wear real earrings is to reflect on the guru's
    knowledge,[15]
    the true One lives in every being's heart.
Through the guru's words, we merge with the
    imperceptible,
    spontaneously attain its pure reality.
Seekers who serve, discover.
    Nanak: no other action succeeds.
They recognize the order, the wondrous order,
    see the true way for beings to be.
Clear of ego, free, they hold truth within,
    we call them yogi.

From the imperceptible, the pure manifested,   24
    the formless took on forms.
The true guru's insight leads to the supreme state,
    merges us with the true word.
They cast off dualities of I-me,
    realize the One is truly one and true,

true yogis recognize the guru's sacred word,
    their lotus within blooms bright.
Dying to the ego, they see it all. All is within,
    they nurture empathy for all beings.
Nanak: they receive honors,
    they see their self in everyone.

25 Born from truth, merging in truth,
    truth and true beings are one and the same.
The false enter the world and find no refuge,
    stuck in duality they come and go.
The guru's sacred word ends their cycles,
    the One assesses and blesses.
Damaged by dualities,
    we lose our taste for the name's elixir.
Only those the One inspires get it,
    they are set free by the guru's word.
Nanak: they let go of I-me dualities,
    the swimmer carries them across.

26 Those who face the self, forget the awe of death,
covet others' possessions, pile up losses.
Deluded, they wander the wilderness,
lost in their evil ways, like chanters of mantras in
    cremation grounds.
Oblivious to the word, they shout obscenities.
Nanak: those colored in truth, know happiness.

27 Those facing the guru are in awe of truth,
they sharpen the dull with sacred verse.[16]

Those who face the guru sing praises of spotless Hari,
they attain the supreme pure state.
Focused on Hari with each and every pore,
Nanak: those who face the guru are merged in truth.

Those facing the guru relish reflecting on the Vedas,[17]   28
they gladly carry others across.
Those who face the guru bask in knowledge of the sacred
    word,
they relish the experience of the inward path.
Those facing the guru find the invisible infinite One,
Nanak: they reach the door of liberation.

Those facing the guru think and tell the untold,   29
support their families,
murmur the love within,
live by the sacred word.
They know and make known the mystery of the word,
Nanak: burning their I-me, they merge within and
    without.

Those who face the guru know truth created the earth[18]   30
on which the game of creation and destruction is staged.
Dyed in the colors of the guru's word,
they soak up truth and go home in honor.
There's no honor without the true word.
Nanak: without the name,
    how can we be with truth?

31 Those facing the guru gain all wisdom and the eight *siddhi*
        powers,[19]
    the truly aware swim across the world-ocean.
    Those who face the guru can tell good ways from the bad,[20]
    can distinguish attachment from detachment.
    Those who face the guru swim across, carry others along,
    Nanak: they are released by the sacred word.

32 Colored in the name, they have no I or me,
    colored in the name, they stay absorbed in truth,
    colored in the name, they reflect on the yogi's way,
    colored in the name, they reach freedom's gate,
    colored in the name, they learn of the three worlds,
    Nanak: colored in the name, they rejoice forever.

33 Colored in the name, they converse with siddhas,
    colored in the name, they practice unbroken discipline,
    colored in the name, they live the essential truth,
    colored in the name, they reflect on knowledge and virtue.
    Without the name, all talk is vain,
    Nanak: all glory to those colored in the name.

34 The perfect guru gifts us the name,
    the way of yoga is to be absorbed in truth.
    Yogis stumble in their twelve schools,
        renunciates, in their six and four.[21]
    Only those who die to live
        in the guru's sacred word, enter freedom's gate.
    Without the sacred word all cling to duality,
        look in your heart and see.

Nanak: the blessed among the blessed,
    keep truth in their heart.

Attentive, those who face the guru attain the jewel   35
and know how to assess its value.
Those facing the guru earn through true actions,
their mind trusts in truth.
If the One is pleased, they see the unseen,
Nanak: those facing the guru never get hurt.

Those who face the guru   36
    practice charity, recite the name, and bathe,
they focus effortlessly,
win honors at the court,
befriend fear's chief destroyer.
They do good, enable others too
and bring them along, Nanak, to join with the One.

Those facing the guru grasp the shastras, smritis, and   37
    Vedas,
they know the secret of each and every heart.
Those who face the guru let go of hostility and conflict,
erase all calculations.
Nanak: steeped in the color of Ram's name,
those facing the guru
    recognize the husband.

Without the guru, we wander here and there,[22]   38
without the guru, no effort succeeds,
without the guru, the mind is quite on edge,

without the guru, unsatisfied, we devour poison,
without the guru, illusion's snakebite kills us,
Nanak: without the guru, there's loss upon loss.

39 Those meeting the guru get carried across,
their wrongs erased, virtues rewarded.
Liberation and great bliss
    are to reflect on the guru's word.
Nanak: those who face the guru never fail,
in the shop of the body,
their peddler mind deals serenely with truth.

40 Those who face the guru are a bridge built by the one
    designer.
When Lanka's demon kidnapped Sita,
Ramchanda slayed Ravana.[23]
Those facing the guru know Babhikhan's secret,[24]
they carry stones across the sea,
rescue thirty-three crores and more.[25]

41 Facing the guru ends all rounds of rebirth,
those who face the guru are honored in the divine court,
distinguish true from false,
effortlessly fall into contemplation,
dive into praise at the court,
Nanak: those facing the guru are free of fetters.

42 Those who face the guru gain the pure name,
they burn I-me with the sacred word.
Those facing the guru praise truth,

they remain absorbed in truth.
The true name wins them the highest honors,
Nanak: they see through the whole multiverse."

"What's the source of life?   43
    What's the teaching for these times?
Whose disciple are you?
What's the story that keeps you so free?
Listen Nanak, young fellow,
give us your thoughts on the story
of how the word takes you across the ocean of the world."

"Breath is our beginning, and this is the time[26]   44
    for the true guru's teachings.
The word is my guru
    my awareness the disciple
        attuned to it.
I live free telling the untold story.
Nanak: through the ages,
    the cow-minding Gopal is my guru,
the story I focus on, the one sacred word.
Once you face the guru, egoism just burns away."

"How can one chew on iron with teeth of wax?   45
What diet can flush out pride?
How to have clothes of fire in a house or temple of snow?
Where's the cave where one can live in balance?
Who is known to permeate here and beyond?
What thought attunes the mind to itself?"

46 "Expel the me-me and I-I inside,
  erase duality, become one with the One.
  Self-facing fools find the world harsh,
  but living on the sacred word, we can chew iron.
  Know the One both inside and out,
  Nanak: the true guru's will puts out the toxic fire.

47 When we soak in awe of truth, pride fades away.
  Thinking of the sacred word, the One is known.
  Dwelling in the sacred word, truth is found in the heart.
  Body and mind are cooled by the color of love,[27]
  toxic fires of lust and anger doused,
  Nanak: our lover gazes upon us with love."

48 "How can the mind retain the ice-cold moon's shade?[28]
  How can the blazing sun keep it ablaze?
  How can the face of death,
    an incessant spy, be turned away?
  What wisdom sustains the honor
    of those who face the guru?
  Who is the warrior who slays death?
  Think it through, Nanak,
    give us your response."

49 "If you say the sacred word,
    infinite light floods the mind,[29]
  the sun enters the moon's house,
    darkness disappears.
  Anchored once in the name,
    joy and sorrow become the same.

It is the One who takes us across the shore.
The guru's insight fills the mind with truth,
this way, Nanak begs, death won't eat us up.

The name is the ultimate essence of meditation,   50
without the name, pain and death sting.
When real merges into real, the mind rejoices,[30]
dualism withers, the One enters our house,
breath bursts into melody, the skies burst into thunder,
Nanak: spontaneously, we meet the immutable.

Void within, void without,   51
    sheer void, the three worlds.
If you know of the fourth state,[31]
    vice and virtue have no effect.
If you know the mystery of void in all hearts,
you are as the timeless Purakhu, pure god.
Nanak: those colored in the color of the pure name,
are themselves the maker Purakhu."

"All speak of the void over and over,   52
how did this unstruck void come to be?
What are they like who are absorbed in it?"
"They are just like the One who created them,
unborn, they do not die,
    they do not come or go.
Nanak: the guru-facing train their mind.

Where the nine lakes fill up   53
    and overflow into the tenth,[32]

the unstruck void blows the trumpet.
By truth created, they tangibly see,
the truth that surges in each and every heart.
The hidden sacred verse revealed,
Nanak: they discern truth itself.

54   To meet spontaneously in love is bliss.
Awake, those who face the guru do not sleep,
they hold on to the word's infinite void,
chanting the word, they free themselves and their friends.
The guru's teaching steeps them in truth,
Nanak: their ego goes, they join
      never to drift apart in doubt."

55   "Where's the place to dispose of foul thoughts?
Why is ignorance of reality injurious?
None can rescue those tied to the door of death,
without the sacred word, there's no honor or respect.
Nanak: how will those clueless self-facing fools
learn to go across?"

56   "Foul thoughts vanish by thinking of the guru's word,
meeting the true guru is the door to liberation.
Blind to reality, the self-facing burn,
ripped by ignorance, they injure themselves.
To follow the will is all virtue and wisdom,
Nanak: it wins honors in the court.

57   Stock of truth their wealth,
they go across and take others along.

Serenely rapt, enlightened, honored,
none can assess their worth.
Wherever I look there's the One,
Nanak: the love of truth takes us across."

"Where dwells the sacred word they say   58
    that carries us across the world-ocean?
What supports the breath
    that flows the distance of the three and seven
    fingers?[33]
How to be still while you speak and play?
    How can you see the unseen?"
"Listen master, Nanak begs you, truly
    try to train your mind,
we face the guru, tune in to the true word,
    the gaze of love reaches us,
the One knower, the One seer,
    luckily unites with us.

The sacred word dwells ceaselessly within,   59
    invisible, it's everywhere before my eyes;
it dwells in the air and in the void,
    formless, the One is in each and every form.
With the gaze of love, the sacred word lodges in the heart,
    inner doubts dispel;
the name lives in the mind, so
    mind and body become sacred as the sacred verse.
The word, 'guru,' carries us over the world-ocean,[34]
    know the One here and beyond;

no features, no complexion, not a shadow of illusion,
    Nanak: recognize the sacred word.

60 Renunciates, true void feeds the breath
    you measure with your ten fingers.[35]
Those facing the guru sing, churn out reality,
    discern the invisible infinite.
As their triple strands vanish, the sacred word settles
    in their mind, free of pride.
Within and without they know only the One,
    they fall in love with Hari's name.
When the unmanifest manifests,
    they realize the three yogic channels,[36]
Nanak: the true guru's sacred word,
    joins them with truth beyond these."

61 "The breath, they say, is the life of the mind,
    but what does it feed on?
What's the currency of knowledge, renunciate?
    What must siddhas live off?"
"Renunciates, besides the sacred word, there's no food,
    the thirst of I-me never vanishes.
Rapt in the sacred word, absorb the timeless elixir,
    live content in truth."
"What's the wisdom that keeps us balanced?
    What diet satisfies?"
"Nanak: experience joy and sorrow alike,
    the true guru ensures death won't eat us up.

Neither flushed with love, nor drunk on elixir,   62
without the guru's sacred word, we sear and scorch.
Semen is not retained, the sacred word not spoken,
breath is uncontrolled, truth unworshiped.
Those who tell the untold and keep their balance,
Nanak: discover Ram deep in their self.

By the guru's grace they blush with love,   63
they get drunk on truth, sipping the timeless drink.
The guru's insight quenches their toxic fire,
drinking the undrinkable, their inner self delights.[37]
Worshiping truth, those facing the guru cross to the other
     side,
but so few, says Nanak, grasp this."

"Where does the elephant mind live?[38]   64
     Where does breath stay?
Where does the sacred word reside, renunciate,
     that settles the straying mind?"
"By the gaze of love the true guru is found,
     the mind moves into its own house.
When ego is eaten up, the self is left pure,
     the racing mind settles down."
"How is the source discerned?
     How is the inner self known?
     How can the sun enter the house of the moon?"
"Those who face the guru expel the I-me inside,
     Nanak: they submerge in serenity.[39]

65   With settled mind still in their heart,
        those who face the guru discern the source.
     Their breath finds home in the navel,[40]
        they find the reality they seek.
     The sacred word lights up the three worlds,
        echoes constantly deep inside.
     Hunger for truth eats up their sorrow,
        satisfied, they live on truth.
     Those facing the guru know the unstruck verse,
        only rare ones realize its meaning.
     Nanak says, praise truth, absorb truth,
        its color never fades."

66   "When there was no heart, no body,
        where did the mind abide?
     When there was no base for the navel lotus,
        where did the breath reside?
     When there was no form or line of any kind,
        who'd be absorbed in the sacred word?
     When there was no frame for blood and semen,
        Who'd measure or evaluate?
     When there was no color, dress, or shape in sight,
        how could truth be seen?"
     "Nanak: for the ecstatic rapt in the name,
        truth and truth alone was then,
        truth and truth alone is now.

67   When there was no heart or body, renunciates,
        the ecstatic mind remained in void.

Without base for the navel lotus,
    breath lived at home in love.
When no form or sign or caste existed,
    the ultimate word lodged in the unborn One.[41]
When earth and skies did not exist,
    the formless One lit up the three worlds.
All colors, costumes, contours came to be the One,
    the one wondrous word.
Without truth, nobody is holy,
    Nanak: this is the untold story."

"How is the world produced, my man?   68
    How will its suffering end?"
"The world is produced by I-me, dear fellows,
    oblivious of the name, it suffers.
Those who face the guru
    focus on the reality of knowledge,
    the sacred word burns off their I-me.
Their body and mind, sacred like the sacred verse,
    are rapt in truth.
Ecstatic in the name and name alone,
    their hearts beat with the truth.
Nanak: without name there's no yoga,
    look into your heart, think about it.

Those who face the guru reflect on the true word,   69
the true verse is revealed to them,
their mind is drenched in love.
    But so few realize this.

Those who face the guru live in their own home,
those yogis discern the real path,
Nanak: those who face the guru,
    know only the One.

70   Without serving the true guru, there is no yoga.
Without meeting the true guru, no liberation.
Without meeting the true guru, we do not find the name.
Without meeting the true guru, we suffer great pain.
Without meeting the true guru, dark pride prevails.
Nanak: without the guru,
    life fails, there is death.

71   Those facing the guru kill their I-me, win their mind.
They hold truth in their heart.
Those facing the guru conquer the world,
    tear Death's messenger to death.
Those who face the guru suffer no defeat in court.
They know the One who joins together,
Nanak: those who face the guru recognize the sacred
    word.

72   Listen, renunciates, my last word on the sacred word—
    without name, there is no yoga.
Rapt in the name, stay drunk night and day.
    The name is bliss.
The name shines light on everything,
    the name gives insight.
Many dress up in robes without the name,
    truth itself leads them astray.

Renunciates, the true guru gives the name,
    only then we master the way of yoga.
Nanak: think about it, look in your mind,
    without the name, there's no escape."

Your limits without limits, you alone know,[42]   73
    what can any of us say?
You hide yourself, reveal yourself,
    you revel in all colors.
Countless saints, siddhas, gurus, disciples,
    search for you by your bidding.
You give them the name they beg for,
    they give their life to see you.
Everlasting Prabhi stages this play,
    those facing the guru realize it.
Nanak: the One is spread across the ages,
    there is no other.

Thematic Compositions

THE HOURS

1

In the first quarter of the night,[1]
   my roving friend,[2]
   we receive the command in the womb.
Turned upside down
   we perform austerities,
   my roving friend,
   we beseech our husband.
We beseech and praise our husband,
   turned upside down,
   rapt in meditation.
Flouting social norms,[3]
   we enter this dark age,
   naked again, we must leave.
We live this life of ours
   as the pen has written on our foreheads.
Says Nanak, in the first quarter,
   my friends,
   we receive the command in the womb.

In the second quarter of the night,
   my roving friend,
   attention wanes.
We're bounced around from arm to arm,
   my roving friend,
   like Krishna in Yashoda's home.

2

From arm to arm the baby is bounced around,
    "This is my child," the mother claims.
Idiotic mind,
    come to your senses,
    nothing is yours in the end.
How can you not know your creator?
    Keep that One's knowledge within.
Says Nanak, in the second quarter,
    my friends, attention wanes.

3 In the third quarter of the night,
    my roving friend,
    we fix on wealth and youth.
We forget Hari's name,[4]
    my roving friend,
    the only escape from bondage.
My friends, we forget Hari's name,
    drown in illusion.
Devoured by wealth, drunk of youth
    we squander our precious life.
We don't deal in righteous stock,
    don't befriend good actions.
Says Nanak, in the third quarter,
    my friends, we focus on wealth and youth.

4 In the fourth quarter of the night,
    my roving friend,
    the harvester comes to the field.
When death grabs us and takes us away,
    my roving friend,
    nobody grasps the secret mystery.

Nobody knows Hari's secret
    when death grabs us and takes us away.
All this wailing for the dead is fake,
    in an instant we turn strangers.
We attain only the object
    we set our heart on.
Says Nanak, in the fourth quarter,
    my friends, the harvester harvests the field.

THE DAYS OF THE LUNAR MONTH

1 First, the One wondrous being,[5]
deathless, birthless,
    without caste or constraint,
unfathomable, imperceptible,
    without form or frame
—search on and you will see
    in each and every heart.
I joyously circle
    those who see and show others.
With the guru's grace
    they reach the highest state.

Without Jagdish, "lord of the world,"
    there's nothing to recall, nothing to recite.
With the guru's sacred word,
    see the divine palace deep within.

2 Second, fall for duality, repent in the end,
you'll come and go tied to death's door.
What will you bring? What will you take?
Death's messenger bashes your head.
Without the guru's word, no one escapes,
there's no liberation in pretentious acts.
3 By combining,
    truth created itself.

Split the egg,[6]
    combined, and split again.
Made the earth and sky,
    places fit to live.
Made night and day, fear and love.
The One who makes, oversees.
There is but one creator, no second.

Third, the One created Brahma, Vishnu, and mighty   4
    Shiva,
gods, goddesses, and many forms.
Who can count the kinds of light?
The One who creates, knows their value,
it knows their value, for it flows in them.
Is that One close or distant? Who can say?

Fourth, the One created the four Vedas,   5
four sources, diverse languages;[7]
created eight and ten,[8]
    six and three.[9]
Only those the One enlightens
    can understand.
They live in the fourth stage
    beyond the three,[10]
Nanak prays to be their slave.

Fifth, five spectral ghosts dance out of step,[11]   6
while unseen Purakhu is free.
Some of us full of doubt and desire,
    go hungry and thirsty.

Some stay satisfied,
   sipping the elixir of the sacred word,
Some are dyed with passion,
   others are dead dust,
While some stand in the courtly mansion
   in its ever-present sight.

7   Liars have no honor, no name.
A black crow never turns pure.
A bird caught is put in a cage,
stays behind bars, without escape.
The husband alone sets us free,
the guru's insight fortifies devotion.

8   Sixth, six the philosophies Prabh set up,[12]
while the unstruck word plays soundless.[13]
At Prabh's wish, invites come from the palace
where those the word pierces are honored.
Different guises burn and wear the wearer out,
truthful living merges the true ones with the truth.

9   Seventh, a true and content body
brims with seven seas of pure waters.[14]
Its bath, moral behavior,
   its focus, truth in the heart.
The guru's sacred word
   helps carry everybody across.
Truth in the mind,
   love of truth in the mouth,

marked with truth,
    nothing gets in the way.

Eighth, train mentally and gain   10
    the eight *siddhi* powers.[15]
Worship sovereign truth with actions,
forget about air, water, fire,
focus on the pure true name.
Absorbed in it,
    a mind is never devoured by death,
Nanak prays.

Ninth, we name nine masters, nine planets,[16]   11
but the strongest master lives in every heart.
This whole world is mother's offspring.[17]
Greet Prabh, timeless protector—
at the beginning, across the ages,
is, and will be that limitless One who can do anything.

Tenth is the name, giving, bathing.[18]   12
Bathe night and day
    in truth's knowledge and virtues.
Slime leaves truth untouched,
    doubts and fears wash away.
It takes but an instant
    for brittle thread to snap,
you know, this world is no different,
keep your mind fixed on truth,
    revel in its colors.

13   Eleventh, bring the One inside your heart,
     see off violence, craving, and lust,
     enjoy the fruit of ritual fasting,[19]
        see yourself, the self you are,
     not by hollow acts can you see the real,
     with no need for food, pure, utterly free,[20]
     the pure true self is pure forever.

14   Wherever I turn I see only the One
     who created so many beings
        in manifold designs.
     If we cling to fruit alone,
        we lose the fruit of our actions.
     If we overindulge in sweet and sour,
        we lose our true sense of taste.
     False greed greedily laps up the greedy,
     living truthfully,
        the guru-centered stay free.

15   Twelfth are the twelve zodiac signs
        the renunciates keep in mind.[21]
     Night and day they stay awake,
     alert in rapt adoration,
        they never sleep.
     The guru is delighted,[22]
        death cannot eat them.
     Wholly detached,
        their enemies defeated,
     they steep in love,
        Nanak pleads.

Twelfth, learn to be kind and giving,   16
bring back your outward-going mind,
keep the fast to give up craving,
sing the silent song in your mouth.
It's just the One in the three worlds,
    you know,
realize the truth—
    that's purity and discipline.

Thirteenth, a tree beside the sea   17
if rooted in ambrosia
    towers in love and crosses over.[23]
It doesn't wilt in fear, nor does it sink.
Without divine awe,
    it drowns and dies in shame.
With divine awe in the heart,
    the heart in divine awe,
we sit on the throne, cherished by truth.
Fourteenth, enter the fourth stage of bliss.   18
Destroy the strands of time—
    passion, inertia, and truth.
Bring the sun into the house of the moon,
gain the value of doing yoga.
    Immerse yourself
    in the One spanning
the fourteen worlds, netherworlds,
galaxies, and constellations.

New moon night: 19
    the new moon hides in the skies,

find it, scholar,
    search the sacred word.
As the moon up in the sky
    lights up the three worlds,
the creator creates and creates,
    and watches over its creation.
Those who truly see with the guru's help,
    join with the One,
The forgetful, self-facing,
    just keep coming and going.

20 Set up home and hearth
    on the lovely, steady spot,
accept the true guru
    to realize the One within.
We wreck ourselves with hopes,
the bowl of dualist cravings shatters.
Those released from the trap of attachment,
Nanak prays to be their slave.

SONG OF THE TWELVE MONTHS

Listen, we reap the fruits of our past deeds.[24]   1
Joys and pains are for everyone,
    and given by you, are good.
Yours is the whole creation, Hari,
    what's in my paltry power?
    Hari, I can't live without you
    for a second.
Without my lover I suffer
    friendless, alone.
    With the guru before me,
    I drink ambrosia.
Anything done with Prabh in mind,
    active creator yet formless,
    is work well done.
Nanak: she watches the way for her lover,
    hear her, Ram,
    her very being.[25]

The *bābīhā* calls for her lover,   2
    the *koel* sings his praise.[26]
She savors all the pleasures, that woman
    in her lover's intimate embrace.
If she pleases him, Hari embraces her.
    A blessed wife,
her body a lofty palace with nine doors,
    Murari comes to live
    in her own home.

"I'm all yours, you're mine, my beloved,
    night and day, I'm colored in your love."
Nanak: the *bābīhā* cries "beloved, beloved,"
    the *koel* is made lovely by the sacred word.

3 Hear me, Hari, bathed in my lover's love
mind and body soak and steep in you,
    unable to forget you for an instant.
How can an instant slip?
    I offer myself to you,
    I live only to sing your praise.
No one belongs to me and I belong to no one,
    without Hari, I cannot live.
I seek your support, Hari,
    by living at your feet, my body is pure.
Nanak says, vision grows wide, comfort deep,
    and the mind is centered by the guru's sacred word.

4 Ambrosial drops drizzle down exquisitely.
Easy and effortless is meeting with her prized friend,
    she's in love with Hari.
He enters her temple when she pleases him,
    the virtuous woman is elated.
In every home the husband and blessed wives revel,
    why then does he forsake me?
Clouds are cast low in the sky,
    rains enthrall,
    mind and body are soothed by love.
Says Nanak, when the ambrosial verse drizzles,
    the gracious One enters our home.

Chet's spring glows with bumblebees,[27]   5
the barren woods of Bar bloom,[28]
    how I long for him to return home.
If her husband fails to come
    her body wilts in the pain of separation,
    how can she be happy?
The *koel* sings in the mango grove,
    how can I bear the ache inside?
Bees buzz beside blossom boughs,
    mother, how can I live in this deathly state?
Nanak: in the month of Chet,
    joy surges, if the wife finds her husband
    Hari at home.

The month of Vaisakha is glorious,   6
    branches dressed up in their finest,
while she watches for Hari at her door.
    "Please have compassion and come,
come home, beloved,
    take me across the impassable ocean.
    Without you, I am worth less
    than half a cowrie shell;[29]
once you like me, my value grows immeasurably.
    If I could see you, I'd show others too, my love.
You're not far I know,
    you're inside I feel—
    I recognize Hari's palace."
Nanak: in the month of Vaisakh,
    Prabhu is to be found,
    once the mind is conscious of the sacred word.

7   The month of Jethu is glorious.
     How can one forget the beloved?
The land burns like an oven,
     the woman pleads.
She pleads and remembers his virtues,
     she earns Prabh's approval.
He lives detached in the true palace,
     but only if he allows may I enter.
Lowly and helpless without Hari,
     how can I gain the joys of the palace?
Nanak: in Jethu she realizes the One is her,
     her virtuous actions succeed.

8   The month of Asarhu is glorious.
     The sun blazes in the sky,
the earth suffers agony,
     the heat scorching like fire.
Sap is sucked dry,
     smoldering death for all,
     still the sun's work goes on.
The sun's chariot races on,
     while she looks for shade,
     crickets drone in the woods of Bar.
She who piles up misdeeds,
     faces suffering ahead.
     She who gathers truth,
     receives happiness.
Nanak: those blessed with such a mind,
     live and die steeped in Prabh.

It is Savana, reach out, my mind—　　　　　　　9
　　the clouds have burst
　　the monsoon is here.
My mind and body long for him,
　　but my husband is away in foreign lands.
He's not coming home,
　　I am sighing to death,
　　lightning strikes me with fear.
Alone in bed, alone I lie in sheer pain,
　　mother, this suffering is death.
Without Hari, how can there be sleep or hunger?
　　What clothing can soothe the skin?
Nanak: the wife is lucky to be
　　in her husband's embrace.

In the month of Bhadon she is lost in delusions　　　10
　　and regrets in her brimming youth.
Water and land are awash
　　in the roaring revelry of the season.
Rain sheets the dark night,
　　how can a young woman find joy?
　　Frogs croak, peacocks screech,
bābīhās cry "beloved, beloved,"
　　snakes go biting about,
mosquitoes sting, lakes flood,
　　but without Hari, where's the joy?
Nanak: I will ask my guru the way to go,
　　where Prabhu is, there we must go.

11 In the month of Assu, beloved,
     come to me,
     this woman is dying in sorrow.
She'll meet him only if Prabh wants to,
     but if she pursues duality she's lost.
Wrecked by lies,
     abandoned by her husband,
     her hair will fade like reeds in bloom.
With summer behind,
     the cold season ahead,
     my mind trembles at this passage.
In all ten directions boughs are bursts of lush green,
     but that alone is sweet that ripens on its own.
Nanak: come meet me in Assu,
     my beloved,
     the true guru will be our go-between.

12 In the month of Kattak we are bid
     to do as Prabh wishes.
A lamp burns steadily
     lit with reality
as oil to the lamp is the beloved to his bride,
     who, soaked in joy,
     lights up at their union.
False deeds end in false death,
     virtuous deeds lead to death's end,
     liberation.
Devotees of the name live in their true home,
     they hold you at the center of all hopes.

Nanak: please open the door and meet me,
    an instant's wait feels like six months.

The month of Magghar is glorious,   13
    if beings dip deep in Hari's virtues.
A virtuous woman enjoys her virtue,
    her immutable beloved is pleased.
Immutable, all-knowing, wise is our maker,
    while the whole world whirls about.
Knowledge, contemplation, virtues—
    beings immerse in them
    only if Prabh so desires.
I have heard songs, music, the words of poets,
    only Ram's name
    puts sorrow to flight.
Nanak: a wife her husband dotes on,
    is utterly devoted in her love.

In the month of Pokh frost comes,   14
    sapping life from blades of grass to thick forests.
Why don't you come,
    you who live in my mind,
    my body, my mouth?
Mind and body enjoy Jagjivan,
    I revel in the guru's sacred word.
Born from egg, womb, sweat, or earth,
    your light pulsates in every heart.
Grant me a glimpse,
    giver of compassion,
    give me the insight to become free.

Nanak: a wife in love with Hari,
    revels in the reveling colors of her reveler.

15 The month of Magha is pure,
    water crossings are seen within.[30]
Find the beloved spontaneously,
    immerse in virtues,
    and find yourselves embraced.
Listen, beloved, my handsome Prabh,
    if my body soaks up your virtues,
    I will please you,
    I'll bathe in the sacred waters.
The Ganga, Jamuna, their confluence with Sarasvati, and
    the seven seas[31]
    will be my sacred dip.
My charity, almsgiving, and worship are Paramesaru,
    the one supreme ruler known across time.
Nanak: in Magh our supreme joy is to remember Hari,
    that's our immersion in the sixty-eight water
    crossings.

16 In the month of Phalguna, my mind is rapt in love,[32]
by night and day it's rapt,
    the selfish self is gone.
Mental craving is cast out,
    just as you wished,
    be kind, now come home.
I could dress up in so many ways,
    without my beloved
    I will find no place in the palace.

Necklaces, ribbons, perfumes, silks adorn me
    only if my lover seeks me.
Nanak: the guru brought them together,
    the wife found the husband
    in her own house.

Twelve months, seasons, dates, and days,   17
    all are glorious,
if hours, minutes, seconds tick naturally
    toward the true One.
I have met Prabh, my beloved,
    my actions have succeeded,
    the creator knows best.
The One who adorns her, loves her too,
    together, they enjoy their union.
Glorious the bed in her home as her beloved revels,
    facing the guru, her forehead shines with fortune.
Nanak: day and night the woman enjoys her lover,
    ever the blessed wife of husband Hari.

SONGS OF MOURNING

1 Come meet me, my friends,[33]
    let us take the true name together.
We mourn parting from this body,
    let us recollect the Sahib instead.
Recall the Sahib, keep our eyes on the path,
    we too must walk on.
The One who makes, is the One who takes,
    all that happens is its will.
What we sow here we reap later,
    there is nothing we can command.
Come meet me, my friends,
    let us take the true name together.

2 Death would not have such a bad name
    if people knew how to die.
Let us serve our mighty Sahib,
    so the way ahead turns easy.
Let us walk the easy way, reap the fruit,
    and meet with praise ahead.
Let us bring our offerings and join with truth,
    our honor written in the records.[34]
Let us enter the palace, beguile our husband,
    revel in radiant colors.
Death would not have such a bad name
    if only people knew what it is.

The death of heroes is worthwhile,   3
    if it wins approval.
Heroes in the hereafter are those
    who gain true honors in the divine court.
Honored at court, they depart with dignity,
    no pain touches them thereafter.
Meditation on the One earns reward,
    serving the One makes fears depart.
Not proud, with self-contained mind,
    they are known to the knower.
The death of valiant heroes is real,
    their death wins approval.

Nanak: what's there to mourn for, Baba?   4
    This world is sheer magic.
Our sovereign watches over all it makes,
    reflects over its creation.
It thinks over its creation and sustains it,
    the One who makes is the One who knows.
It sees, perceives, recognizes its command,
the maker knows its making,
    all this is its infinite form.
Nanak: what's there to mourn for, Baba?
    this world is sheer magic.

VERSES ON EMPEROR BABUR

1

1 Khurasan was attacked, Hindustan terrorized.[35]
Our creator gives no blame,
    had the Mughal descend as death's emissary.[36]
When the victims' cries rent the air,
    did you not feel their pain?

Creator, you belong to all of us equally.
If the mighty fight the strong, I'm not upset.

2 But when a burly lion attacks a flock of sheep,
    their master must be questioned.[37]
This jeweled country is now a ravaged bitch,
    no one to care for her dead.
You tear apart, and you join the broken,
    we marvel at your wonders.

3 They give themselves grand titles,
    indulge in all they fancy,
our husband looks on them as worms,
    gnawing away at bits of grain.
When we die to the I-me, we live, we win,
    Nanak: we sing your name.

2

1 Once they had luxurious braids,[38]
    and auspicious vermilion in their part.[39]

Now, here they are, hair chopped off with scissors,
    throats choked with dust.
Once they enjoyed the sanctum of palaces,
    now they can't find a corner to sit on.

We bow to you, Baba, we bow.
Timeless purakhu, there's no end to you,
    you watch the scenes you create endlessly.

At their wedding,   2
    their handsome grooms sat beside them.
Alighting from palanquins, adorned with ivory,
    the brides were welcomed to their new home.
Water jars were passed round over their heads,
    sparkling fans waved in attendance.[40]

Each time they sat countless coins were poured,   3
    and each time they stood up, too.[41]
Feasting on coconuts and dates,
    they reveled on their beds.
Today ropes chain their necks,
    their pearl necklaces ripped apart.

Wealth and beauty, their sources of joy,   4
    turned into archenemies.
Soldiers were ordered
    to carry away their ravaged bodies.
If it pleases you, you praise us,
    if it pleases you, we are punished.

5   Had they earlier thought of you,
      would they have met this punishment?
  Lost in fun and games,
      rulers forgot their senses.
  Now with Babur's rule declared,
      even princes have no bread to eat.

6   Some lost their time for prayer,[42]
      some their rite of worship.[43]
  Their sacred kitchen squares defiled,
      how will Hindu women put on their holy dot?
  Those who never remembered Ram,
      cannot utter *Khuda* now.[44]

7   Some made it back from the battlefield.
      People flocked asking about loved ones,
  for some it was written
      that they'd sit down and cry.
  Only what pleases you takes place,
      Nanak: we humans are helpless.

3

1   Where are the sports, the stables, the horses,
      the kettledrums, and woodwinds?[45]
  Where are the sword belts, the chariots,
      the bright red uniforms?
  Where are the lustrous rings, those lovely faces?
      Nowhere to be seen no more.

This world is yours, you are our cowherd.
In an instant you can undo your creation,
wealth tearing brothers apart.[46]

Where are the mansions, gates, palaces, pavilions,　　　2
　　those fabulous caravanserais?
Where are the women on those luxurious beds,
　　whose beauty stole sleep forever?
Where are the betel leaves, the sellers, the harems?
　　All vanished like shadows.

For wealth's sake, countless were ruined,　　　3
　　for wealth's sake, countless led astray.
Wealth never comes without misdeeds,
　　it does not follow anyone at death.
The creator led them astray,
　　took away their morals.

They heard of the king's invasion,[47]　　　4
　　those countless *pīrs,* yet they failed to stop him.
Lasting abodes and sturdy temples razed to the ground,
　　princes hacked to pieces lay mounded in dust.
Not a single Mughal went blind,
　　no spell worked.[48]

Mughals and Pathans fought,[49]　　　5
　　their swords clanged in the battlefield.
Mughals aimed and fired guns,
　　Pathans attacked with elephants.

If their credentials were ripped in court,
    my friends, they had to die.

6 Women—Hindu and Turk, Bhatt and Thakur,[50]
some had their veils torn from head to toe,[51]
    others made the crematorium their home.[52]
Their husbands did not return home,
    how did they pass their nights?

7 You creator are the doer, the cause of all our doing,
    who do we go to, to speak our suffering?
Our pain and joy rest in your will,
    where else can we go to cry?
As your order orders us, you delight.
    Nanak: we get what is written for us.

4

1 Know it Lalo, this is the husband's sacred verse[53]
    as it comes to me.[54]
From Kabul he descended with his evil wedding party,[55]
    asked for gifts by force, Lalo.
Beauty and morality have gone into hiding,
    falsehood presides over all, Lalo.
Qazis and Brahmans have lost their sway,
    it's Satan who reads marriage contracts now, Lalo.
Muslim women read the Qur'an,
    in pain they call for Khuda, Lalo.
High- or low-caste Hindu women
    reckoned the same writing, Lalo.

Wedding songs are written in blood,
    blood is worn as saffron, Lalo.[56]

Nanak sings the Sahib's glory,   2
    from the city of the dead he judges.[57]
He who creates colorful games,[58]
    watches, sitting apart, alone.
True is the Sahib, true his justice,
    he judges with true reasoning.
This body will become frayed and tattered,
    then Hindustan will heed these words.
They came in seventy-eight, they will go in ninety-seven,
    then a disciple of humanity will rise.[59]
Nanak speaks the true sacred verse, he tells the truth,
    truth is what the times call for.

ALPHABET ON THE WOODEN BOARD

S

1 Singular, the Sahib is the only One[60]
    who designed this whole creation.
Those who serve who realize it,
    make their life a success.

Why do you forget, my foolish mind?
Brother, count yourself literate
    only when you hand over your account.[61]

I

2 Incipient is the giver,
    it is truth itself.
If the guru-centered see it in this script,
    their errors recorded are erased.

U

3 You must praise the One
    who has no limit.
Its servants attain the fruit,
    they live truthfully.

Ṅ

Knowledge—those who see through   4
    are learned pandits.
They see the One in all beings,
    don't talk of I-me.

K

When curls turn white   5
    and shine without soap,[62]
the king of death arrives with his spies,
    drags people chained to illusion.

Kh

Creator, the great emperor of the world, 6
    buys us for a price and pays us wages.
His grip holds the whole world tight,
    there's no other commander.

G

If we give up the song of the cowherd Gobind,[63] 7
    all our talk is vain.
Remember, the One who designs the clay jars,
    makes also the kiln in which to bake them.

Gh

8 Diligent devotees serve diligently,
   holding firm to the guru's sacred word.
   They see no difference between pain and joy,
   Sahib is pleased this way.

C

9 The One who created the four Vedas,
   each of the four sources, the four ages,[64]
   is the ascetic yogi across the ages,
   the *bhogi* who enjoys the sources,[65]
   is the learned pandit.

Ch

10 Shadows come and go within us,
   our delusions are your doing too.
   You produce them in us, get us lost in them,
   by your doing, we join the guru too.

J

11 This beggar for knowledge
   has begged for eighty-four lakh lives.[66]
   The One alone takes, the One alone gives,
   I have yet to hear of another.

Jh

Why kill yourself with anxiety, my people?　　　12
　　The One gives whatever it wants.
As the One gives, sees, commands,
　　so we receive our livelihood.

Ñ

The gaze of love shows me　　　13
　　there is no other.
The One dwells everywhere,
　　the One lives in my mind.

Ṭ

Why be tyrants, my people?　　　14
　　We could depart at any moment.
Don't gamble your life away,
　　run for refuge to Hari's lap.

Ṭh

They keep their inner self serene,　　　15
　　their consciousness rests at Hari's feet.
Ever mindful, they swim across,
　　you bless them with happiness.

Ḍ

16 Why deceive one another, my people?
        All that exists must depart.
    Attain happiness by serving the One,
        who lives equally in each of us.

Ḍh

17 The One destroys what it creates,
        does whatever it wants.
    As the One does, sees, commands,
        it frees all those it looks on with love.

Ṇ

18 Know the hearts the One lives inside
        sing Hari's praise.
    The creator unites them to itself
        and frees them from rebirth.

T

19 This bottomless world-ocean
        has no end in sight.
    I cannot swim, I have no raft, I am drowning,
        my royal savior, take me across.

Th

There is no place or space without the One.   20
    All that is done is its doing.
What can we doubt or call illusion?
    Whatever the One likes is good.

D

Don't let us blame others,   21
    blame sprouts from our own actions.
We reap as we sow,
    let's not blame others.

Dh

Who animates the cosmos with its force,   22
    who colors everything,
that's the giver we get every bit from,
    every action we do, hinges on its will.

N

He spends all his time with his other wives,   23
    I've neither seen nor grasped him.
I call myself happily married, sisters,
    yet I've never met my husband.

P

24 Our emperor, supreme ruler Paramesaru,
      designed this world for the delight of sight.
    The One sees, recognizes, knows everything,
      dwells inside us and out.

Ph

25 This full world is trapped in the noose
      tied tightly by death's chain.
    Only they are rescued with guru's grace,
      who run to seek Hari's refuge.

B

26 The One began to play *caupari*[67]
      on a game board forged of the four ages.
    With all created beings its pieces,
      the One rolled the dice across.

Bh

27 They who seek, gather fruit,
      awestruck by the guru's grace.
    But self-centered fools go around, oblivious,
      spinning in eighty-four lakh circles.

M

Attachment, mortality, Madhusudan,[68]
    we remember this when we die.
With so much else packed in the body,
    the letter "m" slips away.[69]

28

Y

Yes, there's no more birth
    if we realize truth.
The guru-centered speak, see, know
    only the One.

29

R

The One resides within every being,
    as many as it creates.
The One creates all beings, hands us our tasks,
    yet only with the name within us do we succeed.

30

L

The One who leads us to our tasks,
    seduces us with sweet illusions too.
The order of its will,
    accept all food and all drink equally.

31

V

32 Indwelling god Vasudeva, supreme ruler Paramesaru,[70]
    takes on various forms to experience them.
Present within and without,
    the One sees, tastes, knows everyone.

Ṛ

33 Why wrestle and squabble, my people?
    Fix your gaze on the One who's everlasting.
Focus on the One, unite with truth,
    offer yourselves to the One.

H

34 Here is no other giver who
    creates and feeds all living beings.
Focus on Hari's name, unite with Hari's name,
    gain profit on Hari's name night and day.

A

34 Alpha creator got everything going,
    whatever is to be done, the One does.
The One does, makes us do, knows everything,
    there's nothing left for the poet Nanak to say.[71]

THE GRACELESS

Clumsy, chocked with countless flaws,[72]   1
    how can I enjoy the husband, my friend?[73]
Every woman I see is better than the next,
    but who even knows my name?
My companions revel with the husband
    in the shade of the mango tree.
I don't have their virtues,
    who can I blame for that lack?
Can I recount any of your virtues?
    Can I spell any of your names?
I cannot grasp any one of them,
    I offer myself to you forever.
Gold, silver, jewels, colorful gems, and pearls,
the husband gave me,
    I got attached to them.
Mansions of brick, mortar, and stone
    I made my prized assets.
Trapped by their trimmings,
    I did not sit beside my husband.
Now cranes cry out in the skies above,
    white herons have perched down.[74]
But this woman has to go to her in-laws' home,[75]
    how will she show her face?
I slept, slept through the morning too,
    oblivious of the journey ahead.
I parted from you husband,
    all I gathered were sorrows.

You are virtue, I am vice,
    but Nanak has one request:
all these nights are for the happy wives,
    won't you spare just one
      for hapless me, my friend?

THE GRACEFUL

If I have you, I have it all,[76]   2
    Sahib, you are my prized asset, my friend.
Inside you, I live in bliss,
    with you in me, I am cheered by all.
If you say, I sit on glorious thrones,
    if you wish, I'll beg as a recluse.
If you say, seas flood deserts,
    lotuses bloom in the skies.
If you wish, I cross the world-ocean,
    if you wish I drown.
If you say, I revel in the husband's colors,
    rapt in praise of the treasury of virtues.
If you wish, I'm frightened by my husband,
    I come and go in the cycle of death.
You are inaccessible and immeasurable, husband,
    I could collapse saying your praise.
What to ask for? What to say or hear?
    I hunger and thirst to see you.
Find the husband with the guru's sacred word,
    this truly is Nanak's prayer, my friend.

Selections Across
Musical Modes

SIRIRAG RAGA

1

A palace of pearls dazzles with gems,   1
 excites with scents
of musk, saffron, incense, sandal.
Don't let them distract me,
 don't let your name escape my mind.

Without Hari my life is on fire.
I asked my guru,
 realize there's no other refuge.

A floor studded with diamonds,   2
 a bed strung with rubies,
enchanting faces shining with jewels
 flaunt their colors.
Don't let them distract me
 don't let your name escape my mind.

I become a siddha with riches and powers 3
who appears and disappears
 keeping audiences in thrall.
Don't let that distract me
 don't let your name escape my mind.

A sultan with an army, I sit   4
 with my feet resting on a throne,
issuing orders and drawing tax,
 Nanak: all this is but a puff of air.

Don't let that distract me
    don't let your name escape my mind.

2

1 If I lived age after age
        with only air as food and drink,
    sealed in a cave with no ray of sun or moon,
        with no resting place to sleep and dream in,
    I could not gauge your value
        nor utter the vastness of your name.

Formless truth is where you are
—so we hear and say.
        But only if you want us to, we want you.

2 If I were grass cut fine many times over
        or flour ground in a mill,
    burned by fire and turned to ash,
    I could not gauge your value
        nor utter the vastness of your name.

3 If I flew as a bird across a hundred skies,
    and lived, invisible, without food or drink,
    I could not gauge your value
        nor utter the vastness of your name.

4 Nanak: if I read scores of pages
        flowing with love many times over,
    if I wrote like the wind
        with ink that never fails,

I could not gauge your value
    nor utter the vastness of your name.

3

As is written, so we speak   1
    As is written, so we eat
As is written, we walk the path
    As is written, we hear and see
As is written, we breathe the air
    What is left to ask or know?

Baba, illusion's play deceives.[1]
Blinded, we forget the name,
    linger neither here nor there.[2]

Life and death must follow birth,   2
    here death devours us all.
To the place where we sit to learn,
    we must walk alone.
Those left behind weep for us,
    they heap piles of chaff.

All say you're the greatest of the great   3
    no one says, you're any less.
Yet none can gauge your value,
    nor does mere talk make you more.
You alone are the true Sahib,
    the rest of us your creations
    across countless worlds.

4   They, the lowest of the low,
        lower than the lowliest,
    Nanak: I want to be with them.
        Why envy the high and mighty?
    Where the lowly take refuge,
        is the blessing of your loving gaze.[3]

4

1   Greed is a dog, lies, a sweeper,
        deceit devours corpses,
    slander stuffs the mouth with dirt,
        anger is low-born fire,
    bad taste, self-praise
        these have been my flaws, my maker.

Baba, speak words that win honor.
Good are those called good at court,[4]
    bad ones end up weeping.

2   The taste of gold, the taste of silver,
        the taste of women, the taste of scents,
    the taste for horses, that for palatial beds,
        the taste of sweets, the taste of meat,
    if I stuff my body with these pleasures,
        where will the name find space to lodge?

3   Words that bring us honor,
        carry a seal of approval.
    Bland words shrivel the self,
        hear this, stupid ignorant mind.

Good are those who please the One,
    nothing else need be said or told.
Wisdom, honor, and wealth to them   4
    who hold the One in their hearts.
What praise is enough for them?
    What can embellish them more?
Nanak: those outside the gaze of love,
    enjoy neither charity nor the name.

5

The giver gives us an opium pellet of lies,   1
stoned, we forget death,
    and make merry for a few days.
Sufis who receive the truth,
    live in the divine court.

Nanak: keep in mind, true is the true One.
Serving truth we gain happiness,
    and enter your shrine in glory.[5]

True wine is not made from molasses,   2
    it's made from the true name.[6]
Those who hear and praise it,
    I circle them with joy.[7]
The truly drunken mind
    settles in the divine palace.

Bathing in the virtuous name,   3
    scenting this body with truth,

our faces glow, a gift worth a million gifts.
When in trouble call out to the One,
    the source of all our joy.

4 How can we forget you
    who owns our life and breath?
Without you everything is impure,
    no matter what we eat or wear.
All our talking is a lie,
    only what you like is good.

6

1 Burn all lust, grind it into ink,
    burnish the mind into smooth paper,
with love as pen, awareness the scribe,
    question the guru and write down the answer.
Write the name, write songs of praise,
    keep on writing about the endless One.

Baba, learn to write a record
that will be marked true
    at the place where a mark is required.[8]
2 There they receive praise,
    endless joys, endless delights,
the holy dot glows on their faces[9]
    their minds hold the true name.
Actions win honors, not hot air.

3 So many arrive, so many leave,
    commanders-in-chief, too.

Many are born beggars,
    others command huge courts.
In the hereafter we discover that except for the name
    nothing counts.

Fear of you, fear of the beyond,   4
    my body is wasting away.
Sultans and khans I saw once
    are now turned to dust.
Nanak: once we must get up and go,
    all fake ties tear apart.

7

A good woman radiates her virtues,   1
    a bad one writhes in despair.
If you want your husband, young woman,
    lies are not the way.
No boat or raft will carry you
    to your husband so far away.

My perfect master sits on a steady throne.
Face the guru perfectly,
    gain truth without measure.

Lovely is the temple of Prabhu Hari,   2
    full of jewels and rubies,
a castle of spotless gold,
    covered with pearls and diamonds.
With no ladder, how do you scale the castle?
    Meditate on guru Hari and see.

3 The guru is the ladder, the guru is the boat,
     the guru is the raft that takes us to Hari's name.
The guru is the ship carrying us across the ocean,
     he our river crossing, and our river too.
If he's pleased with me I shine,
     I bathe in the pool of truth.

4 We call the One the most perfect of perfects,
     seated on its perfect throne.
Its perfect places are glorious,
     It perfects the hopes of the hopeless.
Nanak: if we join the perfect One,
     our virtues will only grow.

8

1 You are the enjoyer, you the joy,
     and you are the ravisher too.
You are the bride in her dress,
     and you the groom on the nuptial bed.

My Sahib is colored in love,
     fills everyone with joy.

2 You are the fisherman, you the fish,
     you are the waters and the net,
you are the weight that holds the net,
     you the lost ruby swallowed by the fish.

3 You are myriad colors—
     how my lover glows, my friends.

Look how the happy wife is in perpetual delight,
    and look at us instead.[10]

Nanak humbly offers his prayer: 4
    you are the pool and you are the swan,
lotus in the day and lily of the night,
    and it's you who watches them and rejoices.

9

Maula makes the world bloom,   1
    makes it lush and green.
Blessed is our creator,
    who keeps water and land in balance.

Death comes to all, mullah,
best to stand in awe of our creator.

We call you mullah and *qazi,*   2
    only if you realize Khuda's name.
You may be well-read,
    once life is measured out,
    no one remains.

A true *qazi* abandons his ego   3
    with the one name, his anchor, knowing
our true creator is and ever will be,
    neither born nor dying.

We may do *namaz* five times a day,   4
    we may read the holy Qur'an.[11]

Nanak: when the grave calls us,
    food and drink are left behind.

10

1 With a dog and two bitches,
    barking and barking from daybreak on,
    my lies a knife, my loot a carcass,
    my creator, I lead the life of a wild hunter.

I learn no honor, do no good deeds,
I look scarred and scary.
Your one name rescues the whole world,
it is my only hope, my sole support.

2 My mouth spurts slander day and night,
    eyes pry the home of others,
    this outcaste body seethes with lust and wrath,
    my creator, I lead the life of a wild hunter.

3 With a devil's mind and the looks of an angel,
    a robber who robs the world,
    the cleverer I act, the heavier my load gets,
    my creator, I lead the life of a wild hunter.

4 An ingrate, I don't realize
      your acts.
    How can I show you my face,
      foul thief that I am?
    Lowly Nanak tells you his thoughts,
    my creator, I lead the life of a wild hunter.

11

One consciousness for all living things, 1
none was created without it.
It guides us wherever we walk,
by one written rule we all come and go.

Why try clever tricks, my life?
In giving or taking the One never delays.

All beings are yours, and you are theirs, 2
Sahib, how can you get angry?
And even if you do, still
they belong to you, and you belong to them.

We loudmouths ruin language, yet 3
you weigh us on the scales of your loving gaze.
Perfect wisdom trails good actions,
without good actions, we dip lower and lower.

Nanak begs, 4
      What are the real knowers like?
they recognize their self, realize the One,
think deeply with guru's grace.
They are received at the divine court.

12

You are the sea, all-knowing, all-seeing, 1
      how can I, a fish, find your limits?
Wherever I turn, there you are,
      if I slipped from you, I'd burst to death.

I know neither the fisherman nor his nets,
when I find trouble, I hand it to you.

2 You flow everywhere, yet I think you're far.
All my doings are before you.
You see all I do, still I deny them,
I neither serve you, nor praise your name.

3 Whatever you give is all I eat,
there's no other door to go.
Nanak says one prayer,
this life and body are yours alone.

4 Close up, far away, everywhere, and
in between, it's you.
You see, you hear, you make up the whole world.
Nanak: your wish is our command.

13

1 My mind plays a song of praise,[12]
the more I feel, the more it plays.
To the One we sing our sound of music,
how great is it? Where is its place?
The ones who'd know are all rapt in love.

Baba, Allah is unfathomable and infinite.
His name is pure, his place is pure,
he is our true provider.

How vast is your command?   2
    No one can know, no one can write it.
Even if a hundred poets jointly do their best,
    they can't get a speck across.
No one realizes your worth,
    we say what we happen to hear.

Pīrs, prophets, the faithful, martyrs, devotees,[13]   3
shaikhs, *qazis*, mullahs, and dervishes[14]
reciting *durūd* blessing reach the divine court[15]
    there, they're blessed even more.

You ask no questions when you create or destroy,   4
    you need no advice when you give and take.
You know your power, you act alone,
you watch all with your loving gaze
    and give to them who please you.
We do not know your places and names,   5
    how great is the name of names?
How vast is the place where my emperor lives?
Nobody can reach it, who do I ask?

Among castes you prefer no caste,   6
    even if you make some higher.[16]
Greatness sits in the One's hand,
    you give to whom you please.
By your will alone, you enrich your creation,
    without a minute's delay.[17]

7 Everyone says, "More, more,"
      expecting even more.
  How great is our giver?
      We can't count your gifts,
  Nanak: nothing runs out,
      for ages and ages your stores are full.

14

1 Adorned, we all arrive
      as wives of the one husband.
  In vain, some count and calculate,
      they dress up in red.
  Pretense wins no love,
      fake trappings wreck us.

  Precious Hari, see the husband enjoy his wife—
  the blessed bride entices you, and
      you deck her with your favor.

2 Adorned by the guru's sacred word,
      mind and body draped in the husband,
  she stands, hands folded, eyes fixed on truth,
      and makes her wish.
  She blushes passionately in awe of the true One,
      lives gloriously, colored in its love.

3 Known as her lover's handmaiden,
      this blushing woman embraced the name.[18]
  True love never snaps,
      she's joined with truth forever.

The sacred word she loves, pierces her mind,
    I'd circle her joyously forever.

Joined with the true guru,   4
    this wife will never be a widow.
Her charming lover ever new,
    truth never fades or dies out.
He enjoys this blessed wife forever,
    she stands in the true gaze of love, his will.

She braids her hair with truth,   5
    dresses in clothes of love.
Sandal scents her consciousness,
    seeps into her temple's tenth door.[19]
She lights the lamp of the sacred word,
    the garland of Ram's name resting on her breast.

The woman's beauty shines within,   6
    the jewel of love sparkles on her forehead.
Her beauty and perception gleam,
    she's in love with infinite truth.
She knows no one but her Purakhu beloved,
    she is in love with the true guru.

Sleeping in darkness without her husband,   7
    she tosses the night away.
Her limbs, her whole body, sear in pain,
    mind and wealth on fire.
When her husband does not enjoy her,
    her youth lies wasted.

8 Her husband lies beside her in bed,
    yet the heedless wife slumbers.
Her husband wakes, she sleeps,
    whose advice will help?
Nanak: if the true guru joins her,
    she'll wake up in awe,
    love will be her friend.

15

1 You are the song and the singer,
    you are the listener and the thought,
you are the jewel and the appraiser,
    you are the priceless price.
True One, you are honor and splendor,
    and their giver, too.

Precious Hari, our creator, our maker,
keep us as you please, just give us the way of your name.

2 You:
    pure diamond, deep crimson,
You:
    sparkling pearl,
    the devotee, and the go-between.
We praise you through the guru's sacred word,
    we see you, unseen, in every heart.

3 You are the ocean and the boat,
    you are the shore both near and far,

Wise one, you are the true path,
    the sacred word ferrying us across.
Without awe of you, fear takes over,
    without the guru, we grope in the dark.

We see the creator stand steady,   4
    the rest of us come and go.
You alone are the pure One,
    the rest of us are caught in messy affairs.
Those rapt in truth, stay free,
    sheltered by the guru.

The sacred word shows us precious Hari,   5
    the guru's verse colors us in truth.
A body settled in the house of truth, never soils.
The gaze of love joins us with truth,
    each bond forged by the name alone.

Those who recognize the truth   6
    are happy through the four ages,
no pride, no greed,
    but truth held in their heart.
The one name is the only profit in this world,
    gained with our guru's insight.

Gather the stock of truth,   7
    its capital earns profit forever.
True in devotion and prayers,
    gain a seat at the true court.

In the light of Ram's name,
   our account is settled with honor.

8 You are higher than the highest, we say,
      though none can see or describe you.
   Wherever I turn, I only see you,
      as the true guru showed me.
   Nanak: effortlessly serene,
      we see your steady light.

16

1 Deep in the swirling salty sea,
      the fish didn't see the net.
   So clever and beautiful,
      how could she be heedless?
   Her deeds trapped her,
      death hangs over her head.

Brothers, know that death hangs over us,
careless like fish, we get caught in its net.

2 The whole world is bound to die,
      without the guru, death is proud.
   Those colored in truth escape,
      dispel deceptive dualities.
   The truthful ones reach the true court,
      I circle them with joy.

3 Like hawk for a bird,
      or cage in a hunter's hand,

there is the bait to catch us.
    But if the guru keeps us, we're saved.
Without the name, we're picked up and pitched
    with no friend, no companion.

We say the One is the truest of the true,   4
    true is the place of the true One.
Those who embrace truth,
    who place their mind on truth,
we know their minds and mouths are pure.
    These wise ones face the guru.

I begged the true guru   5
    to unite me with my friend.
I met my friend and I am happy,
    death's men were poisoned to death.
I live in the name, the name lives in me.

It's pitch dark without the guru,   6
    clueless, we lack the sacred word.
Where the guru's insight shines,
    truth takes over,
death dares not tread.
    Light merges into light.

You are our friend, you the all-knowing,   7
    you join us with yourself.
With the guru's sacred word, we praise you,
    never reaching your end.

Where the guru's infinite word chimes,
    death cannot reach.

8 By the will all are born,
    by the will we make a living,
by the will we yield to death,
    by the will we unite with truth.
Nanak: what you want to be will be,
    nothing living beings do is done.

17

1 My mind, pierced with Ram's name,[20]
    can think of nothing else.
Feeling the sacred word brings peace, and
    dyeing in Prabh's passion is supreme bliss.
Keep me as you want,
    all I want is the support of Hari's name.

The husband's will is true, my mind.
Who crafted this body and mind in beauty,
    attend to that One in adoration.

2 I chop my body into tiny bits
    to offer in the sacrificial fire,
make my body and mind fuel
    to keep it ablaze night and day,
pile millions of actions to earn merit
    but nothing works like Hari's name.

My body could be sliced in half 3
    with a saw sliding down my head,
and frozen in the Himalayas.
    Still my sick mind would stay sick.
I've seen how works work
    and dismissed them,
    nothing works like Hari's name.

I donate castles of gold, 4
    offer countless horses and elephants,
give out lots of land and cows to charity,
    my pride and conceit are still in me.
The guru gives true alms,
    a mind pierced by Hari's name.

So many scholars with stubborn minds, 5
    so many Vedas and exegeses,
so many traps to trap us beings,
    the guru-facing alone find the door to freedom.
Truth is higher than everything,
    but higher still is true living.[21]

Hold everyone in high regard, 6
    look down on no one.
The One who molded all these clay jars
    lights the three worlds with the same one light.
Good actions join us with truth,
    this blessing from the beginning of time
    none can erase.

7 When saints meet each other,
> the guru's love inspires peace.
They join with the true guru,
> focus on the tale that cannot be told.
Happy drinking ambrosial elixir,
> they enter the court draped in honors.

8 In every heart a *kiṅgurī* plays[22]
> the lovely sacred word night and day.
Yet so few hear its melody.
> Hone your mind like the guru-facing,
Nanak: clasp the name,
> live out the sacred word,
> Be free.

GAURI RAGA

1

1 Wisdom our mother, contentment our father,
truth our brother—these are our near and dear.[23]

Much as we want to describe it,
we can't ever grasp your creative power.

2 Beauty and awareness, our two parents-in-law,
good actions, our cherished wife.

Nanak: 3
Our meeting is our wedding day
      our wedding, a parting from duality,
Truth, our children.[24]

2

A mix of air, water, and fire, 1
a game of capricious intellect,
with nine doors and a tenth too,
think of it, scholar, figure it out.

The same one speaks, instructs, listens.
Those who know their inner self,
      have the answer.

Breath talks through this body of dust, 2
who is it that dies, then?
      Figure it out, scholar.
Insight, conflict, vanity die out,
but the One who sees, does not.

What we seek on pilgrimages afar, 3
that precious jewel, sits in our heart.
Pandits study and study, argue and discuss,
yet fail to see the thing that exists within.

No, I did not die, the villain in me did. 4
The One who's suffused in us, never does.

Nanak, the guru showed me the ultimate being,
I see no death or birth anymore.

3

1   Night is lost to sleep,[25]
        day is lost to eating.
    This life, a precious diamond,
        goes for a cowrie.[26]

You don't know Ram's name, you idiot,
you'll regret later on.

2   With no love for the infinite One, they
        bury infinite treasures underground.[27]
    Chasing infinite riches they long for,
        they return, the infinite One lost.

3   If we got all we wanted
        how lucky we'd all be.
    Though we long for much more,
        we reap what we sow.

4   Nanak: the One who creates,
        takes care of us too.
    But we'll never know the husband's will,
        who will he honor, who can say?

4

I wish I were a doe   1
    living in the woods,
      eating roots and fruits of my choice.
By the guru's grace, I'd find my lover,
    I'd circle him with joy.

I am Ram's gypsy woman,[28]
your name is my only stock and trade.

I wish I were a *koel*   2
    living among the mango trees,
      serenely thinking of the sacred word.
I'd easily find my lover,
    a vision of infinite beauty.

I wish I were a fish   3
    swimming in the waters,
      seeing the reality of all beings.
To my lover across the shore,
    I'd dash with arms wide open.

I wish I were a she-serpent   4
    snaking underground,
      the sacred word in me, all my fears behind.
Nanak: she's forever the blessed wife,
    light fused in infinite light.[29]

5

1 I freshen up my body with sandal oil,[30]
dress up in silks and satins.
But where's the pleasure
    without Hari's name?

What should I wear?
    How do I dress to display myself?
Where's pleasure without
    Jagdish, who owns the world?

2 Curls dance over my ears,
    pearls caress my neck,
I snuggle in my red quilt with crimson flowers.
But where do I find pleasure without
    Jagdish, who owns the world?

3 This beauty has enchanting eyes,
puts on sixteen adornments,[31]
    looks prettier than ever. Yet
without devotion to Jagdish, who owns the world,
    she's always in despair.

4 On her cozy bed in her palatial home,
gardeners arrange flowers day and night. Yet
without Hari's name, her body aches in pain.

Stallions, elephants, cavalry, musical bands,   5
armies, officers, attendants, ornate displays,
    all false spectacles
without Jagdish, who owns the world.

We may be hailed siddhas,   6
    call up our psychic powers,
wear a crown on our head
    with parasols waving overhead.
Where do we find truth
    without Jagdish, who owns the world?

We may be known as nobles, emperors, kings,   7
bark orders left and right
    all an act.
Without the guru's sacred word,
    no task ever gets done.

The urges of I-me leave with the guru's sacred word,   8
whose insight shows Murari in the heart.
Nanak begs for refuge in your lap.

6

Grasp, by the guru's grace[32]   1
    the problem is over.
The stainless name in every heart
    is my master.

There's no escape without the guru's word.
　　Grasp it, dwell on it,
see to millions of meritorious acts
　　without the guru, darkness prevails.

2　What to say to the blindly ignorant.
　　Without the guru, they can't see the path.
　　　　How'll they ever succeed?

3　The fake they call real
　　　　with no sense of the real's essence,
　　the blind they call assessors,
　　　　look at the marvels of this dark age.

4　They call sleepers awake
　　　　and the ever-awake, asleep,
　　the truly alive they consider dead,
　　　　and the dead, they do not mourn.[33]

5　All who are coming are said to be going,
　　　　all those going are said to come,
　　what belongs to others, they claim their own,
　　　　what is theirs, they don't enjoy.

6　The sweet tastes bitter,
　　　　the bitter, sweet,
　　those colored in the One are scorned,
　　　　this is the scene of this dark age.

Slaves are being served,   7
    nobody thinks of the master.
You won't whip butter
    churning water in a puddle.

Who grasps the meaning of this verse   8
    is my guru.
Nanak: recognize your inner self,
    it's the infinite One beyond.

You grant us everything,   9
    you lead us astray.
Thanks to the guru, we realize
    All this is you
    our ultimate being.

ASA RAGA

1

Cymbals and anklets jangle deep in the heart,[34]   1
the world plays to the beat of the drum,
Narada dances in thrall of the flux of time,[35]
where can steady good people rest their feet?

Nanak lives and dies by the name.
This world is blind, Sahib alone is wise.

2   Disciples eat what the guru serves.
Come home to eat his food,
you could live there eating for hundreds of years,
blessed is the day when they recognize the husband.

3   People see the poor yet feel no pity,
but no one lives without give and take,
the king judges with a bribe at hand,
they call on Khuda yet do not obey him.

4   Nanak: they appear and call themselves human,
but act like dogs—an order also from the court.[36]
If by the guru's grace they grasp,
    they are guests here,[37]
they'll find honor at court.

2

1   Your consciousness and melody? Vast as the sacred word.
    Your body? Vast as visible form.
You are the taste, you the scent,
    mother, there's no other to speak of.

My Sahib is One,
One, brothers,
    It is One.

2   You beat us up, you let us free,
    you give, you take.
You watch over us, rejoice in us,
    you give us your loving gaze.

You do whatever is to be done,   3
  there's no one else.
As you hand out, so we receive,
  all this greatness is yours.

My drunken mind   4
  keeps on drinking deceptive sweet wine
  from the dark-age distiller.
You take on so many different forms,
  poor Nanak says.

3

Wisdom our harmonium, love our tambourine,   1
our mind rejoices in bliss forever.
This is our devotion, austerity, penance,
let's dance with passion, our feet on the beat.

Know divine praise has the perfect beat,
all other dance amuses the mind.

Our cymbals, truth and contentment   2
feet tapping in enduring bliss,
with numinous song our only love[38]
let's dance with passion, our feet on the beat.

Mind and thought always whirl in awe,   3
whether we sit or stand
or lie on the floor,
  realize, this body is but ashes.
Let's dance with passion, our feet on the beat.

4 In the concert of seekers, lovers of learning
    face the guru to hear the true name.
    Nanak says this over and over,
    let's dance with passion, our feet on the beat.

4

1 A milkless cow? A wingless bird?[39]
      A waterless plant?
      All worthless.
    A sultan without salaam is a nobody,
      a room without your name is pitch dark.

Why did I forget? I suffer terribly,
I ache in pain, don't slip away from my mind.

2 Eyes go blind, tongues lose taste,
      ears hear no music in the air,
    feet hobble as we lean on another,
      this is the upshot when we do not serve.

3 Plant letters in the pure garden of the heart,
      water them with divine love.
    All trees bear the fruit of the one name,
      without good deeds, what's there to reap?

4 So many beings, they all belong to you,
      but no one gains without serving you.
    Our suffering and joy hang on your will,
      without your name, our life is nil.

Life is dying to oblivion, living for wisdom,   5
    there is no other way to live.
Says Nanak, you give beings the gift of life,
    keep me just as you wish.

5

Body our priest, mind our loincloth,   1
knowledge, the sacred thread,[40]
    concentration, our *kuśa* grass ring,[41]
praise of Hari's name, our purifying bath.
By the guru's grace we join with the ultimate being.

Pandit, think of the ultimate being this way:
make name your purifying practice,
    name your study, name your code of conduct.

Wear the sacred thread only if you have a light within,   2
wear the loincloth and holy dot to uphold the name.[42]
Here and in the hereafter, these go with us,
seek no other deed except the name.

Choose worship and love, burn off illusion,   3
see the One, seek no other.
Find the reality of the celestial tenth door,
make Hari your mouth, recitation, study, and reflection.

A diet of love chases doubts and fears away,   4
our glorious watchman keeps thieves at bay.[43]
Knowing the one Prabhu as our holy dot,
We see the ultimate being in our heart.

5   Moral codes don't win the One over,
recitations don't give its worth.
Neither eighteen nor four ever solved the mystery,[44]
Nanak: it's the true guru who reveals the ultimate being.

6

1   Only those who serve the master
     by turning toward the guru
are attendants, servants, devotees.
The One creating is the One who destroys,
there is no other beside it.

They reflect on the true name in the guru's word,
those who face the guru are truthful in the true court.[45]

2   Every sincere request, every heartful prayer,
our husband in the mansion hears and cheers,
invites the truthful ones to the throne,
showers them with praise,
     whatever the One does comes to be.

3   All power is yours, you are the court.
The guru's sacred word is your true mark.
Those who follow your order, go in honor,
they bear your true mark, nothing stops them.

4   A pandit reads and expounds on the Vedas,
clueless to the mystery that lies inside.
Without the guru we neither know nor realize,
the truth rejoicing in us is Prabh itself.

What can we say, preach, expound?   5
You alone, One, all-wonderful can know yourself.
Nanak: there's only one door to the court.
    Fed by truth,
those who face the guru make it through.

7

My lamp is the one name,[46]   1
    the oil I pour in it, my suffering.
Its flame soaks the oil,
    my appointment with death is called off.

My people, don't think it's jest,
a tiny spark burns a mound of a million logs to ash.

My leaf dish of rice balls is the long-haired Keshav,[47]   2
    my funeral rite, the true name of our creator.
Past or future, here or in the hereafter,
    the true name is my sole support.

Your praise is my Ganga, my Varanasi.[48]   3
    My king, I bathe my core self in it,
I bathe in the waters of truth,
    soak in your love, night and day.

To feed the ancestors some people offer rice balls,   4
    rolled and eaten up by priests.
Nanak: if only these rice balls were your blessings,
    we'd never stop eating them.

8

1 Her mind a pearl cast in a pendant,
      suspended on the string of breath,
the lovely woman drapes her body in kindness,
      she revels with her beloved.[49]

She is charmed by the lover's countless virtues.
Who can match your virtues?

2 Wearing a necklace of Hari-Hari,
      she shines her teeth with Damodar.[50]
The creator's bracelet around her wrist,
      keeps her mind in balance.

3 The ring on her finger came from Madhu's killer,*
      her silks from Paramesaru, the supreme ruler.
She braids her hair with patience,
      lines her eyes with lustrous Sriranga.

4 Preparing her body as a bed,
      she lights up her mind's temple.
Nanak: the ruler of knowledge gets in bed with her,
      and revels with her.

9

1 Created creatures, we do as the One makes us do.
      What can we say, my brother?

---

* Vishnu, or Madhusudan (killer of demon Madhu).

All that is done is its doing,
    why try clever tricks?

Your command is good, and pleases you.
Nanak, they win honors
    who are immersed in the true name.

Our actions comply with the written record,   2
    your order will not be defied.
Read as written,
    who could erase it?

Those who talk a lot in court,   3
    are called fools in the bazaar.
They won't win the chess game,
    their moves will fail.

Neither literate, scholarly, or far-sighted,   4
    nor ignorant or immoral,
we are but the One's slaves. If moved to praise,
    we live up to being called "human."

10

The young woman says,[51]   1
    "My beloved is the font of all colors."[52]
The thicker her love for him,
    the kinder his for her.
When Prabhu showers compassion,
    lover and beloved master join.

On her lovely bed with her beloved,
    her seven soak ambrosia.[53]
Be kind and generous, my compassionate One,
    I'll sing your praise with true words.
Nanak: look how happy she is to see her beloved Hari,
    the young woman's mind is boundless joy.

2   With lovely eyes, serene, she
        offers a prayer of love:
May my body and mind love Hari
    may I revel in Prabh's union.
Reveling in Prabh's love,
    she prays for Hari's comforting name.
When she sees goodness, she grasps Prabhu,
    her vices leave, she gathers virtues:
I can't live for a minute without you,
    to speak or hear of you is not enough.
Nanak calls out "beloved, beloved,"
    tongue and mind drenched in ambrosial elixir.

3   Friends, sisters, my beloved is a peddler
who deals in Hari's name,
    our precious infinite elixir.
Priceless are true hearts beating with the beloved,
    praised be the bride who pleases Prabh.
Some revel with Hari,
    I stand here crying at his door.
Mighty creator and accomplisher,
    splendor-holding Sridhar, fulfills all tasks.

Nanak: the blessed wife basks in your loving gaze,
    she keeps your sacred word in her heart.

True wedding songs play in my home,   4
    my friend Prabh is here.
He revels with those rapt in love,
    lured by a mind lured by him.
I gave him my mind and caught him, my beloved Hari,
    as he desires, so we enjoy each other.
By the blessed word, my body and mind are now his,
    the ambrosial fruit I found at home.
Intellect, recitations, myriad skills—all useless,
    love is won by love alone.
Nanak: our owner is my friend,
    I am not a stranger anymore.

11

A soundless melody soars   1
    to *rhun jhun* crescendo.
My mind, my mind is colored crimson
    by my lover.
Colored day and night, my ecstatic mind
    rests in a whirling void.
The true guru shows me the unseen,
    my beloved, infinite, timeless Purakhu.
What a deluge of joy as I think
    of Narayan's everlasting posture and seat.
Nanak: ecstatics are colored in the name,
    that soundless *rhun jhun* crescendo.[54]

2 How to reach the unreachable
  in his town beyond reach?
  Do tell us the way.
  Be true and disciplined, cultivate virtues,
  live by the guru's sacred word.
  Live the true sacred word, reach your home,
  receive the treasure of virtues.
  With no trunk, roots, leaves, or branches,
  the One reigns supreme over us all.
  Meditation and austerities are exhausting,
  hatha yoga fails us.
  Nanak: the true guru unveils the mystery, and
  effortlessly, we join with Jagjivan,
  the life of the universe.

3 The guru is an ocean of jewels, a mine
  full of rubies and gems.
  Bathed in its seven seas, this mind shines.
  If Prabh wishes, we bathe in its pure waters,
  focus and attain the five virtues.[55]
  Lust, anger, lies, the poisons of illusion rinse off,
  to let hearts soak up the true name.
  Tides of I-me, greed, lust retreat,
  we greet the protector of the poor.
  Nanak: no pilgrimage matches the guru,
  the true guru, our cowherd Gopal.

4 I search from jungle to jungle,
  sift through each blade of grass.

You made the three worlds,
    this whole universe, everything.
Ever still, you set all things in motion,
    there's not a thing that matches you.
You are the giver, we your beggars,
    we praise no one but you.
Giver, you give us gifts beyond imagination,
    devotion to you brings us abundant treasures.
After much thought, Nanak says,
    we can't be free without Ram's name.

GUJARI RAGA

1

I make your name my sandalwood,[56]   1
    my mind the mortar I grind it on.
I mix in saffron of good actions, and
    worship you in my heart.

Worship is to remember the name,
    without the name there is no worship.

Bathe the mind as we do our deities.   2
Impurities wash off,
    life is clean, free of death.

3 Animals hold such goodness,
  feeding on grass
   they feed us ambrosia.
Without the name, cursed is human life,
  all action worthless.

4 Know the One is close, not far at all,
  ever looking after each one of us.
We eat what it gives us.
  Says Nanak, truth exists.

VADAHANS RAGA

1

1 An addict does not become his drug,[57]
  a fish does not become its water,
but those addicted to their beloved
  become lovers of all.

I offer every bit of myself,
  I offer myself to your name, my Sahib.

2 The Sahib is a fruiting tree,
  ambrosia is its name.
Those who drink it, their thirst is quenched,
  I circle them joyously.

You live among us, 3
    yet I can't see you.
How can I quench my thirst, when
    a wall inside dams the stream?

Nanak: I am in business with you, 4
    you are my Sahib and I your capital.
My mind stops cheating
    when I pray to praise you.

2

The virtuous woman enjoys her beloved, 1
    the virtueless woman weeps;
if only she took up virtue,
    she too would enjoy her beloved.

My beloved is full of bliss,
    why would this wife enjoy any other, my life?

If she strings good actions 2
    on the thread of her mind,
the wife's pendant would be priceless,
    threaded into her consciousness.

I don't walk the way you tell me, 3
    but I say I made it home.
If I don't talk with you, beloved,
    how can I expect to live with you?

4   Nanak: besides the One
        there is no other.
    If she's in love with the beloved,
        he will love her too.

3

1   Peacocks have burst into *rhuṇ jhuṇ* chorus,[58]
        sister, the monsoon is here.
    Your bridal eyes, sharp as daggers,
        make the greedy greedier still.
    I'd shred myself for a glimpse of you,
        I live and die for your name,
    because of you I feel so proud,
        without you, what pride have I?
    Break your bangles against the bed, dear bride,
        along with your arm, alongside the bedpost.
    You've dressed up in so many styles, dear bride,
        yet the groom revels with others.
    There is no jeweler, no bracelet,
        no chime of glass bangle either.
    The arms that don't embrace the husband
        burn in despair.
    All my friends have gone to enjoy the husband,
        scorching me,
        whose door can I go to?
    Mother, I have many skills,[59]
        but none has won me my beloved.
    I braided my hair on each side,
        filled the parting with vermilion,[60]

but when I went ahead, I was not welcomed,
    now I die writhing in pain.
I weep, the whole world weeps with me,
    even birds in the forests weep.
My dualized body alone does not weep,[61]
    it tore me away from my lover.
You came to me in a dream, only to leave me,
    I cried my heart out—
I can't make my way to you, my love,
    I can't send a messenger.
Come to me, blessed sleep
    that I may see my lover.
If anybody spoke about Sahib,
    what would I not offer them? asks Nanak.
I would chop my head to offer them a seat,
    still serve them without my head.
How could I not kill my selfish self, not sacrifice my life,
    when my beloved is estranged from me?[62]

4

Why bathe a body defiled by lies?[63]   1
We bathe ourselves living by truth,
truth within leads to the true One.
But without what's written on us,[64]
    we have no consciousness of truth,
    talking, we waste away.
Wherever we go or sit, we must say what's good
    by the sacred word, written on our consciousness.
Why bathe a body defiled by lies?

2   I spoke the words because
       you made me speak.
   My mind loves Hari's ambrosial name,
   the name enchants my mind,
       my house of troubles collapses.
   At the sound of your command,
       joy suffuses my mind.
   Your gaze is full of love, mine is a prayer
       to you who created your own self.
   I spoke the words because
       you made me speak.

3   We all get turns with our husband
       for the acts we do.
   Don't speak ill of anyone,
       or get into fights.
   Don't run in with the owner,
       that's how we lose our self,
   by competing against our partner,
       we grieve.
   Accept what he gives,
       do as we're told,
       don't talk nonsense.
   We all get turns with our husband
       for the acts we do.

4   The One creates us all,
       gives us its loving gaze.
   No one asks for something bitter,
       we all go for sweets.

Much as we may ask
    and seek what is sweet,
    the husband does as he pleases.
Charity, piety, countless good deeds,
    cannot match the name.
Nanak: those whose actions were blessed
    way back in time, receive the name.
The One creates us all,
    gives us its loving gaze.

5

Be compassionate, I want to sing your name.   1
You created everything, you are in everyone.
Within all beings
    you created yourself,
    to each you assign their task.
Some you set up as kings, others you send out begging.
You make greed and attachment seem so sweet, that
    deceived, we lose ourselves.
Be compassionate forever, I want to sing your name.

Your name is true forever, my mind loves it so.   2
All pain is gone, joy fills my being.
Gods, humans, the cultured, the wise sing to you
they sing to you,
    they enchant your mind.
But the oblivious ones, seduced by illusion,
    fritter their whole life away,
ignorant fools don't realize, whoever comes must leave.
Your name forever true, my mind loves it so.

3 Your timeless time is glorious,
     your sacred verse, ambrosial.
Your servants serve you, full of love,
     these people have a taste for you.
They have a taste for you,
     they received your elixir.
Colored in your name, their joy multiplies.
Till the One is tasted,
     all actions, morality, self-discipline are tasteless.
Your timeless time is ever glorious,
     your sacred verse, ambrosial.

4 I circle the true name joyously.
Your sovereignty will never fail,
your sovereignty is immutable,
     it will never fail.
Your servants serve you
     merged effortlessly in you,
no enemy or sorrow touches them,
     no vice dares approach them.
I circle joyously forever
     your one and only name.

5 For eons upon eons we've been your devotees
we sing your song at your door, master.
We recite the One,
     the true Murari,
only when you dwell in our mind.
You made us doubt and forget, you set us free.

By guru's grace, be kind,
    release us from death's clutches.
For eons upon eons we've been your devotees.

My vast Sahib,   6
    unknown, infinite,
how shall I make my request?
    I don't even know what to say.
Look on me with your loving gaze
    I wish to see the truth.
I see truth and know I am yours,
    you make me see you,
pain, hunger, worldly doubts dissolve.
Nanak humbly says, doubts leave,
    the guru's teaching shows
how vast our Sahib is:
    unseen, infinite.

Your eyes are beautiful, your teeth, sparkling,   7
your nose, lovely, your hair, long,
your dazzling body, cast in gold
a golden form with Krishna's rosary.
    Meditate, my friends.
We escape death standing at the gate,
    listen to this teaching, my friends:
Cranes turn into swans,
    mental fetters shatter.
Your beautiful eyes, your sparkling teeth.

8 Your gait delights, your voice beguiles,
   like a cuckoo's song, your youth pulsates.
   Your vibrant youth delights you,
       and we fulfill our mind's desires.
   Like an elephant you sway with every step,
       drunk with your own self.
   Colored in your splendid colors, Sriranga,
       drunk, I flow like Ganga waters.
   Nanak humbly says, I am Hari's slave.
       Your gait delights, your voice beguiles.

SORATH RAGA

1

1 If I please the One,[65]
   I get to sing, and win my reward.
   I win my reward,
   the One sings in me.

   My mind, the guru's words bring treasure,
   stay steeped in truth this way.

2 My guru's insight woke me,
   my restless intellect stopped dead.
   The dazzle of the guru's insight
   banished all darkness.

A mind devoted to the guru's feet,   3
chases away death's every step.
A sense of fear wins the fearless One,
serenely, we return home.

Says Nanak: those attentive realize,   4
the greatest feat in this whole world
is to sing the song of praise,
the One becomes one with us.

DHANASARI RAGA

1

My life sears over and over,[66]   1
the more it sears, the more it wastes.
A body that lets go of the sacred verse,
cries crippled with pain.[67]

Too much talk is useless,
the One knows us without our talk.

The One who shapes our ears, eyes, and nose,   2
gives us our tongue to speak fluently,
nourishes our mind in the heat of the womb,
plays with our breath so we all talk and go about.[68]

3 Attachments, cravings, thrills,
    are all black stains of blame.
    Go with faces stained with them,
    you'll have no place to sit at court.

4 Actions bear fruit saying your name,
    holding on, we swim across,
       there is no other refuge.
    Your name rescues even the drowning,
    Nanak: truth gives to all.[69]

2

1 Praise of a thief does not impress,
    nor does his abuse leave a scratch.
    No one vouches for a thief,
    a thief's actions are never good.

Listen, my dirty blind dog of a mind,
The true One knows without us speaking.

2 A thief may be good-looking,
      a thief may be wise,
    a counterfeit coin is worth barely a cent:
    If placed among the real,
    look, and it's caught.

3 As we do, so we earn,
    we eat but what we sow.
    Self-praise impresses ourselves alone.
    As awareness leads, so we go.

Rubbish, lies, and libels   4
may please the wide world,
but if you are pleased,
    even half-wits win you over.
Nanak: the all-knowing knows all.

3

This body is paper,   1
    the mind, written command,
yet the naïve do not read
    the writing on their forehead.[70]
Their record of the three strands[71]
    gets written out in court,
counterfeits are deemed useless.

Nanak: if there's silver in it,
everybody says, "It's real, it's real."

The *qazi* tells lies,   2
    he feeds on dirt.
The Brahman exploits others
    while he bathes himself.
The yogi is blinded,
    he does not see the way.
All three are bound to ruin themselves.

Real yogis discern the way: 3
by the guru's grace
    they know the One.

Real *qazis* flip over:
by the guru's grace
    they die to their ego to come alive.
Real Brahmans think of the ultimate being,
they hold the whole family as they cross over.

4   The wise bathe their hearts clean
    Muslims wash their wrongs away
    Perceptive readers are welcomed,
    the court's sign is on their foreheads.

4

1   Those times are gone.[72]
      No yoga, no sense of truth,
    sacred places are turning profane,
      the world is drowning.

In this dark age
    Ram's name is the sole reality.
Impostors
    close their eyes, hold their breaths
    cheat the world.

2   They shut their nostrils with three fingers,[73]
      say they can see the three worlds.
    They've no clue who's right behind them,
      how odd their lotus pose.[74]

3   Kshatriyas gave up their moral duty,
      took up the tongue of foreigners.[75]

Society has slipped into the same caste,
    the one devoid of morality.

Pore over eight adornments,[76]   4
    scrutinize Puranas, study the whole Veda,
without Hari's name, there's no escape.
    That's what slave Nanak says.[77]

5

The guru is a sea full of jewels,[78]   1
saints stay close, collecting ambrosia.
Prabh delights as they sip Hari's elixir.
In this sea, swans find their life giver.

What's a poor crane doing bathing in a puddle?
Sinking in filth won't clean it.

The mindful pick each step they take,   2
leave off dualities, take to the formless One,
taste Hari's elixir, and gain their precious freedom.
In the guru's care, no more coming and going.

Swans do not leave this sea   3
serenely steeped in loving devotion.
The swans are in the sea, the sea in them
they tell the untold tale,
    celebrated in the guru's words.

The one yogi sits in the whirling void,   4
neither male nor female, impossible to describe,

absorbing light from the three worlds,
the true refuge of gods, humans, and masters.[79]

5 This font of bliss, holder of the helpless
guru-facing devotees serenely think of.
The lover of devotees dispels their fears,
their I-me goes, they walk the path together.

6 In spite of all efforts, death torments us,
it's stamped on us when we enter the world.
This precious birth withers in dualities,
blind to the self, deluded, we cry.

7 Speak, read, hear the One,
hold to the holder of the earth, Dharnidhar,
    grow patient and virtuous.
The heart grows chaste, true, self-disciplined,
once the mind settles in the fourth state.

8 Dirt does not touch the true and the pure.
The guru's sacred word dispels doubts and fears.
Timeless and unique their form and image,
Nanak begs to be with these icons of truth.[80]

TILANG RAGA

1

1 I make one request, creator,[81]
    please hear me:

truth Haqq, great Kabir, merciful Karim,
    you are our flawless, provider Parvadgaru.[82]

This world is a fleeting stop,
    know this for sure, my heart.
Seized by the hair by Azrael,[83]
    you still know nothing, my heart?

Spouse, children, parents, relatives,   2
    no one will offer you their hand.
When you lie flat at the final *takbira,*[84]
    no one will hold you back.

Day and night beguiled by greed,   3
    lost in vile thoughts
I've failed to do any good.
    This is my state.

A miserable tattler,   4
    blind, oblivious, shameless,
I'm still your devotee, says Nanak,
    dust from your servants' feet.

2

Your awe is my opium,   1
    my awareness, its pouch,
I am a crazy vagabond.
My cupped hands stretch out
    hungry to see you.
I beg at your gate, day after day.

Seeing you present
    I perform samā,[85]
I beg at your gate to receive alms.

2 Saffron, hibiscus, musk, and gold
        adorn each body they touch,
    the radiance of your devotees, though,
        spreads sandal scent on all.

3 Purified butter and silk are never blamed,
    so too your devotees, whatever caste they be.
    They bow in rapt adoration of your name,
    Nanak seeks alms at their door.

3

1 My husband does not like my outfit,
        body steeped in illusion,
        dress dyed in greed.
    My beloved, how can this wife
        enter her nuptial bed?

To my merciful Meharvana
    I sacrifice myself.
To those who remember your name
    I sacrifice myself.
To those who remember your name
    I sacrifice myself,
        a hundred times over.

If my body were a coloring vat,   2
    my beloved, the name, crimson dye,
and the dyer my Sahib,
    such a color would be beyond sight.[86]

Those who dye their clothes in love,   3
    have the husband always nearby.
Nanak makes his request,
    may I receive the dust off their feet?

You create us, you color us,   4
    you give us your loving gaze.
Nanak: when the wife entices her husband,
    he revels with her in rapture.

4

My naïve one, why so proud?   1
Why not enjoy Hari's colors in your house?
The husband is so close, you silly wife,
    why look outside?
Line your eyes with divine awe,
    dress up in love's finery,
you'll be known as the happy wife,
    with whom the husband falls in love.

What can a naïve young woman do   2
    if the husband doesn't love her?
She may lament piteously,
    but still won't make it to the palace.

Without good deeds,
    we gain nothing
    however frantically we run.
Naïve woman,
    drunk with avarice, greed, and pride,
    drowned in illusion,
you won't make it to him this way.

3   Go now to the happy wives and ask them
    how they enticed the husband.
Whatever he does, accept it as good,
    forget all other tricks and loyalties.
Lay your awareness at his feet,
    his love is precious wealth.
Do what the husband says,
    give him body and mind,
    may this be your perfume.
Sister, his happy wives say this is the way,
    to win the husband.

4   By losing the ego we entice our husband,
    no other trick will do.
Write down the day he gives you the loving gaze,
    a wife wins nine treasures.
Loved by her husband,
    blessed with brothers,[87]
    Nanak: she is a happy wife.
Colored with passion,
    drunk on serenity,
    day and night she is rapt in love.

Beautiful, radiant, intelligent,
    she is truly wise.

SUHI RAGA

1

Yoga is not a patched robe,[88]   1
    yoga is not the staff,
    yoga is not smeared ashes,
it's not the earrings,
    nor the shaven head,
    yoga is not blowing the *siṅṅī* horn.
Living purely among impurities,
    we master the way of yoga.

Yoga is not mere talk.
Those who see with the same eye,
    realize everyone is equal,
    they alone are yogis.

Yoga is not visiting tombs or cemeteries,   2
    yoga is not going into trance,
yoga is not drifting off in faraway lands,
    yoga is not bathing on pilgrimages.
Living purely among impurities,
    we master the way of yoga.

3 The guru gifts, and our doubts dispel,
        frantic chasing stops,
    the inner fountain flows, serene melody crescendos,
        we find the One in our house.
    Living purely among impurities,
        we master the way of yoga.
4 Nanak: to live dead to the ego
        is the practice of yoga.
    When the yogi's *siṅṅī* horn blows unblown,
        we reach the fearless state.
    Living purely among impurities,
        we master the way of yoga.

2

1 Which scales, which weights,
        which goldsmith to summon?
    Which guru, which teaching to seek?
        Whom to approach to assess you?

    My passionate beloved,[89]
        I can't perceive your limits—
    you flow in the waters, on land, across space,
        you infuse each one of us.

2 My mind the scales, awareness the weights,
        service to you, my goldsmith,
    deep in my heart, I weigh you.
        This way my awareness remains in balance.

You are the indicator, the weights, the scales,   3
    you are the appraiser.
You observe, recognize,
    you are the dealer.

Blind, base, alienated, this mind of mine   4
    flits from here to there.
Nanak keeps it company,
    how can this fool reach you?

3

The One creates, then watches,[90]   1
    sets the world about its tasks.
The moon lights up the bodies,
    your gifts light up our hearts.
The moon's light—Hari's gift,
    dispels despair and darkness.
The virtuous wedding party glows,
    with the groom chosen
    by the attractive bride.
The wedding went off with great pomp,
    the five sang the sacred word.[91]
The One creates, then watches,
    sets the world about its tasks.

I joyously circle   2
    my dear enlightened friends.[92]
My body is bound to theirs,
    our thoughts fused.

We have honored each other,
    how can I forget these dear friends?
I see them and rejoice,
    I'll hold on to them with my life.
Day after day they display virtues,
    never a single vice.
I joyously circle
    my dear enlightened friends.

3   If there's a jar of perfume,
        let's open it, and breathe its fragrance.
    If good friends possess virtues,
        let us imbibe and share.
    Let's share virtues and walk together,
        leaving our wrongs behind.
    Let's don silks and finery,
        and take our place in the arena.[93]
    Wherever we sit, let us speak justly,
        stir up the elixir and drink it.[94]
    If there's a jar of perfume,
        let's open it, and breathe its fragrance.

4   The One does everything,
        who else would we ask?
        There is no other doer.
    We'd go over to ask if the One forgets,
        go and remind, if it forgets
    but does the creator ever forget?

The One hears, sees, gives
  unimaginable gifts
  without our asking.
Nanak: the giver gives us gifts,
  the designer of the world, truth itself.
The One does everything,
  who would we ask?
  There is no other doer.

BILAVAL RAGA

1

Is it a compliment if I call you "Sir,"[95]   1
  when you are our sultan?
My guide, I go with what you allow.
  A fool, I know not what to say.[96]

Give me the insight to sing your praise,
so I may live in truth by your will.

Whatever happens is by your doing,   2
  all is known to you.
I do not know your limits, my Sahib,
  blind that I am, what intelligence do I have?

What can I say? The more I say,   3
  the more I realize, I cannot tell of the untold.

What pleases you is all I can say,
    a sesame seed before your greatness.

4 So many dogs, I am a stray one,
    barking to sate this body.
  Nanak may lack devotion, even so
    the husband's name stays on with me.

2

1 With my mind a temple, my body a hermit's robe,
    my heart, a pilgrimage ford for bathing,
  and the one sacred word my breath,
    I won't return to the circle of life.

Mother, my mind is pierced with love
    for the compassionate One.
No one else can know my pain,
I cannot think of another.

2 Unfathomable, unknowable, unseen, infinite,
    do take care of us
  you abound in waters, on land, across space,
    your light shines in every heart.

3 All teaching, wisdom, enlightenment
    are yours, yours all temples and shelter.
  My Sahiba, I see none else but you,[97]
    I sing your glory constantly.

All beings seek refuge in your lap,   4
      all care for us rests with you.
Whatever pleases you is good,
      this is Nanak's sole appeal.[98]

3

You are the sacred word and the sign   1
you are the listener and you the science,
you create and survey your creation.
Giver, we obey your name.

Give me that stainless godly name,
I beg to know you, unseen, unknown.

Illusion seduces like a vile woman,   2
an ugly woman, she casts her spells.
False power and image last but four days
the gift of the name lights up the dark forever.

Give up your taste for her,[99]   3
      and doubts dispel.
With a father known,
      a child is not illegitimate.
We belong to the One,
      what's there to fear?
The creator creates, and makes ourselves create.

Dying in the sacred word,   4
      mind overcomes itself.

It stays steady, truth takes over.
I circle the guru, know nobody else.
Nanak: colored in the name, we're carried across.

4

1   Wishes follow what the mind says.[100]
It dictates:
    do good now, now bad.
Illusion's drink quenches no thirst,
the mind is sated and free
    drunk on the true One's love.

Seeing muscles, wealth, spouse,
    why be proud?
Except the name, nothing goes with us.

2   Follow the mind, indulge in pleasures,
wealth goes to others,
    this body turns into a pile of dust,
dust into dust, this whole expanse.
Only the sacred word shakes off dirt.

3   False are songs, melodies, rhythms,
arise from the three strands,
    and disappear.
Dualistic thoughts inflict chronic pain.
Those who face the guru escape,
    their cure: sing divine praise.

We may wear a sparkling loincloth,   4
    holy dot, beads around the neck,[101]
but if there's anger inside,
    scripture is read like a script for a play.
Forget the name and drink illusion's wine:
no devotion to the guru,
    no joy anywhere.

Into pig, dog, ass, cat,   5
beast, low, outcaste, polluted,
facing away from the guru,
    we go on migrating.
Wound up in circles,
    all come and go.

Serve the guru, seize your treasure.   6
Hearts holding the name, triumph forever,
they're not questioned in the true court.
Accept the command, succeed at court.

Join the true guru, get to know the One,   7
Abide by the will, recognize the command,
recognizing the command, reside in the true court.
The sacred word destroys death and rebirth.

Live free, know that all belongs to the One.   8
Hand body and mind over
    to the One who owns them.
No more coming, no more going,
Nanak: true knowers join with truth.

MARU RAGA

1

1 Actions, the paper, mind, the ink,[102]
    good and bad, both get written.
As our actions take us, so we go,
    Hari, your virtues go on and on.[103]

Totally oblivious, you idiot,
unmindful of Hari, your virtues are going off.[104]

2 Night is a trap, day is a trap,
    as many traps as seconds.
Pecking at your bait, you enjoy each day,
    fool, how will you escape?

3 This body a furnace, the mind an iron grill,
    five fires rage within.[105]
Fueled by vile coals,
    they're lapping up the mind,
      while tongs of anxiety feed their blaze.

4 Joining the guru,
    charred iron can turn into gold.
The One gives the elixir of the singular name,
    Nanak: this body revives.

2

1 In pure waters of a pure pond,
    lotus and scum grow.

The lotus befriends scum and water,
    yet remains untouched, untroubled.

You frog, you'll never learn,
in pure waters, you live on dirt.
    Don't you taste the elixir all round you?

In the waters   2
    a lotus, a hovering bee
    humming in praise,
    drunk with its scent.
A lotus lily too senses the distant moon,
    elated, bows her head.

Get clever, frog,   3
    suck the elixir,
    a blend of sugar, milk, and honey.
You don't give up your ego,
    no more than a flea gives up sucking.

Living with pandits, a fool   4
    listens to the *āgamas* and shastras.[106]
Like you, he can't drop his love of ego,
    as a dog can't straighten his tail.

The fake can't enjoy the name,   5
    devotees can't leave Hari's feet.
We do what was written before,
    Nanak's tongue murmurs the name.[107]

3

1   Some call me ghostly,[108]
        some call me off-key,[109]
    some call me human, Nanak,
        I'm just a poor fellow.

Crazy for my king,
        Nanak, I've gone mad.
I know nobody apart from Hari.

2   Obsessed with divine awe,
        are those possessed.
    Apart from the one Sahib,
        they know no other.

3   Possessed are those
        who slave solely for the One.
    They see the husband's will,
        it's all they care to know.

4   Possessed are those
        who fall in love with the Sahib.
    They see themselves as bad,
        the rest of the world as good.

4

1   The One true truth,[110]
        no other.
    You design, you dismantle

As you will, so we live.
    Who could ever deny you?

You create, you destroy   2
you allot each their task.
You think of us, give us virtues
    you lead us on our paths.

You are the wise, you are the seer.   3
You create and cherish your creation
You are air, water, fire.
    You unite. You are the union.

You are the moon, the sun,   4
    the perfect of the perfect,
you are knowledge, contemplation, the guru, the hero.
If we plunge in truth,
    death nor death's net ever touches us.

You are man, you are woman,   5
you are the chessboard,
    you are the playing pieces,
you stage the world arena,
    you judge how each game is played.

You are the bee, the flower, the fruit, the tree,   6
you are the waters, the lands, the seas, and lakes,
you are the crocodile and the tortoise, and yet
    our doer, we can't see you in any form.

215

7 You are the day, you are the night.
 You delight in the guru's sacred verse.
 From the beginning of time,
   the soundless sacred word
   beats in our hearts, by your will
   day and night.

8 You are the priceless jewel,
   matchless in beauty.
 You are the appraiser,
   our perfect weigher.
 You test and bless.
   The One gives and takes, my brothers.

9 You are the bow, and you the archer.
 You are intelligent, beautiful, and wise.
 Speaker, author, listener,
   how creative is your creation.

10 We know air is our guru, water our father,
 the unifying womb, our mother earth,
 night and day,
   two male and female keepers.[111]
   This is the way
   you keep the play of the world playing.

11 You are the fish, you the net
 you are the cow and her protector.
 All beings in this universe are your light,
   Prabhi, they go by your bidding.

You are the ascetic yogi,   12
    you the enjoyer *bhogī*,[112]
you the reveler of ultimate union.
Silent, formless, fearless,
    rapt in trance yourself.
Species and languages converge in you,   13
all we see comes and goes.
But true merchants and traders see through,
    as the true guru shows.

The perfect true guru reveals the sacred word,   14
truth flowing through all of art.
Untouchable, forever carefree,
    not a speck of greed touches you.

Death and life go insane[113]   15
seeing drunk serene hearts
    savor the sacred word.
Giver of freedom and fulfillment,
    you love your devotees who love you.

Pure One, with the guru's insight   16
    we grasp you.
All that exists flows back into you.
Lowly Nanak begs at your door,
    hand me the glory of your name.

5

You are the earth, the bull below it, the skies above[114]   1
You reveal your true virtues.

Celibate, virtuous, content,
    the doer of all that's being done.

2 You watch as you keep creating,
no one can erase your true writing.
You do, you make us do,
    you magnify all we do.

3 Five mischievous thieves lead perception astray,[115]
eyeing the homes of others, they don't look into their own.
This city body crumbles in a heap of dust,
    without the sacred word, we lose respect.

4 Through the guru they see through the three worlds,
they fight off cravings, wrestle with their mind.
Those who serve you, grow like you, fearless One.
    Since they were children,
    you've been their friend.

5 You are the heavens, the middle, everything below,
you are the embodiment of ever youthful light,
your form with dreadlocks is terrifying,
    though really you have no form or feature of any kind.

6 Vedas and Kateb do not know your mystery.
You have no mother, father, son, or brother.
You raise all the mountains and flatten them too,
    yet the unseen is never seen.

So many friends, I am worn out,   7
yet none wriggles me out of my wrongdoings.
The crown of gods, humans, and masters,
    our Sahib gives love,
    and all fears disperse.

You set lost wanderers back on track,   8
make us forget, make us aware.
I see nothing except the name,
    which gives a sense of your reality.

Ganga, Jamuna's playground, Kedara,[116]   9
Kashi, Kanchivaram, Puri, Dwarka,[117]
the Ganga's meeting with the sea,
    the triple confluence,
    sixty-eight sacred sites,
    all are a part of your body.

You are the siddha, the seeker, the thinker,   10
You are the ruler, and you the maker of the five.
Seated on your throne, impartial Prabhu,
    you dispel delusions, dualities, and dread.

You are the *qazi*, you the mullah.   11
The infallible One never forgets.
Merciful, compassionate, generous,
    you have no enmity toward anyone.

You honor those you bless,   12
give to each of us without a speck of greed.

Utterly free, boundless abundance,
    everywhere hidden and seen.

13 How do we praise you,
    inaccessible, infinite,
our true maker, Murari?
Those on whom you gaze with love,
    unite with unity itself.

14 Brahma, Vishnu, Shiva
stand at your gate to serve you,
    unseen, infinite.
Countless others you can see
    crying at your gate,
    their numbers beyond counting.

15 True your praise, true your sacred verse,
in Vedas or Puranas, we see no other.
Truth is my capital,
    I sing a song to truth.
    I've nothing else to lean on.

16 Age upon age truth
    has been, is, and ever will be.
Who has not died? Who will not?
Rapt in you, lowly Nanak
    wishes to see your palace.

6

Age upon age darkness abounded.[118]   1
No earth, no skies,
   only infinite will prevailed.
No day, no night,
   nor moon or sun,
   absolute void meditated on its own.

No species, no languages,   2
   no air, no water,
no creation, no destruction,
   no coming, no going,
no continents, no underworlds
   no seven oceans, no rivers or flowing waters.

No celestial, terrestrial, or underworld,   3
no hell, no paradise, no death, no time,
no heaven or hell, nor birth or death,
   nobody to come or go.

There was no Brahma, Vishnu, or Shiva,   4
the One alone, none else to be seen.
No woman or man, no caste or birth,
   nobody to feel any pain or joy.

There were no holy men or women, nor forest dwellers,[119]   5
no siddhas, seekers, or home dwellers,[120]
no yogi, no wandering *jaṅgam,* no attired figure,[121]
   nobody called Nath.

6   No recitation, sacrifice, self-discipline,
        no fasting or worship,
    nobody there to speak of another.
    You were creating, rejoicing
        as you appraised yourself.

7   No ablutions or austerities,
        no *tulasī* rosaries.
    No cowgirls or Krishna,
        no cows or cowherds.
    No Tantra practices or mantra sounds,
        no pretense.
    Nobody played the flute.[122]

8   No actions or morality,
        nor illusion's greedy fly.
    No caste or birth,
        nor eyes to witness.
    No net of craving,
        nor death written on the forehead,
        no one to focus on anyone.

9   No slur, no seed, no being, no life,
    neither Gorakhnath nor Matsyendra,[123]
    no form of knowledge or meditation,
        no clan or birth,
        no counting for accounts.

10 No distinction of class or looks,
        no Brahmans or Kshatriyas,

no gods, no temples,
 no cows, no Gayatri chant,
no fire rituals of *homa* or *jaga*,[124]
 no bathing on pilgrimage,
 nobody to perform worship.[125]

There was no mullah, no *qazi*,   11
no shaikh, *masāiku,* or *hājī,*[126]
no subjects and no king, no worldly I-me,
 nobody to address or be addressed.

There was no love or devotion,   12
 no Shiva or Shakti,
no friends, no companions,
 no sperm and no blood.
You were the banker, you were the trader,
 as truth desired.

There was no Veda, no Kateb,   13
 no smriti, no shastra,
no reading out of the Puranas,
 no sunrise or sunset.
Speaker and reciter were one and the same,
 the unknown unseen seeing itself.

As you desired you created the world,   14
effortlessly, you unfurled the whole expanse.
You created Brahma, Vishnu, and Shiva,
 you spread illusion and attachment.

15 Only a few hear the guru's sacred word.
You watch as you create,
    each thing is under your will.
You started planets, constellations, and spheres below,
    what was hidden began to show.

16 Who can know your limits?
Only the perfect guru reveals.
Rapt in truth, Nanak, the awestruck
    sings your glory in wonder.

BHAIRON RAGA

1

1 Outside your purview is nothing.[127]
You create, watch, and know each one of us.

What's ours to say?
Nothing whatsoever.
    All that is, is your will.

2 All that is done is done by you.
Is there any other to call upon?

3 We sing and hear your sacred verse,
your wondrous doings you know yourself.

You do, you make us do, and you know us too,   4
Nanak: you keep watch on all you do and undo.

2

Eyes see no more, the body is too weak,[128]   1
    old age has won, death hovers.
Without truth, there's no beauty, love, or joy,
    how to escape death's trap?

My people, remember Hari, life is passing by.
Without the true sacred word
    there's no escape, life wastes away.

Lust, anger, pride, attachment   2
    beset the body with terrible pain.
The tongues of those centered on the guru
    taste Ram's praise,
        this is the way across.

Ears go deaf, intellect wanes,   3
    they don't grasp the serene sacred word.
Blind without the guru,
    the self-facing lose this precious life.

But the ecstatic live serenely focused,   4
    detached, without hope amid all hope.
These free guru-facing, Nanak humbly says,
    remain rapt in Ram's name.

BASANT RAGA

1

1 The happy month of months is here, *mumārakhī*,[129]
    in its ever springlike splendor.
Blossom, my awareness,
    cherish Gobind, everlasting protector.[130]

Naïve fellow, forget your I-me self,
dispel your I-me, learn my mind
    to extract virtues' essence.
2 With actions your tree,
    Hari its branches, morality its flowers
    knowledge bears fruit.
Absorb its thick leafy shade,
    mental pride will fade this way.

3 Eyes see creative power,[131]
    ears hear the sacred verse,
    mouths speak the true name,
focus is serene,
    glorious honor is fully yours.

4 As months and seasons move on,
    keep an eye on what you do.
Nanak: the guru-facing do not wither,
    drenched in Hari, they're green forever.[132]

2

The season is here in its luscious spring, 1
a riotous burst of colors,
    all excited about you.
Who do I worship?
    Whose feet do I touch?[133]

I am the slave of your slaves, I say, my king.
Life of the universe, Jagjivan,
    I know no way to reach you.

Your image is one, 2
    your forms, infinite.
Which of these do I worship, offer incense to?
No one has found your limits,
    where are they?
I am the slave of your slaves, I say, my king.

Yours are the sixty-year cycles,[134] 3
    yours are all the pilgrimages,
yours is the true name,
    supreme ruler, Paramesaru.
We cannot gauge your unconditioned condition,
utterly unknown, we sing your name.

What can poor Nanak say? 4
Everyone praises the same One.
Nanak bows at their feet,
joyously going around each of your names.[135]

3

1 A kitchen made of gold, golden utensils,
  elaborately drawn in silver
      the lines of its sacred square.[136]
  Water from the Ganga, fire of oblation,
  succulent food, cooked in milk.

  Nothing counts, my mind,
  until you soak in the true name.

2 The ten and eight written could be right beside,[137]
  we could recite the four Vedas by heart,
  bathe on special days, pay alms to each caste,[138]
  fast ritually day and night.

3 *Qazi,* mullah, or shaikh,
  Yogi, *jaṅgam,* ochre-robed ascetic,
  or householders doing jobs,
  all those who do not realize,
      are driven away in chains.

4 Actions are written on each forehead,
  we are judged by the actions we've done.
  Ignorant fools order others about,
  Nanak: glory abounds only in the true One's stores.

4

1 Your illusion, alluring, enchants the worlds,[139]
  it's you I see all over, and none else,

you are the master of masters, the god of gods.
Serving at the guru's feet, we receive Hari's name.

My beautiful, deep, profound love,
infinite One, you feed us all,
    yet only the guru-facing sing Ram's name.

Without saintly people, no Hari's company.   2
Without the guru, limbs get dirty.
Without Hari's name, we can't be clean.
The true ones praise the guru's sacred word.

Our keeper, those you care for,   3
you unite with the true guru,
    you treasure them.
You release their toxic I-me traps,
you end all their suffering, Ram the ruler.

Hari's praise conditions this body to perfection,   4
guru's insight reveals the jewel of Hari's name.
Steeped in the name that dispels duality's spell,
devotee Nanak joins with the guru, guru Hari.

5

Listen, sisters and friends, listen   1
    about love.
My lovely beloved is with me, but
how to express the inexpressible One?
The guru has revealed ruler Ram's presence.

Let's get together sisters and friends, and foster Hari's virtues.
Play as a wife with husband Hari Prabh,
*   face the guru, seek and keep him in your mind.*

2 Woeful, a self-facing wife has no clue
the One we all love revels in every heart.
Steady, a guru-facing sees god is with her,
strengthened by the guru, she recites the name.

3 Without the guru,
        no devotion or love.
Without the guru,
        no company of saints.
Without the guru,
        the fumbling blind cry out.
Pure the mind of the guru-facing,
        its dirt all cleansed by the sacred word.

4 Join the guru, win the mind,
day and night, enjoy the yoga of devotion.
Sitting with guru's saints, all troubles depart.
In the yoga of serenity,[140]
        devotee Nanak weds husband Hari.

6

1 When you worship the holy *sālagrāmu,* Brahman,[141]
        make good deeds your *tuḷasī* beads.[142]
Anchor your boat in Ram's name,
        seek compassion from the compassionate One.[143]

Why waste life irrigating alkaline land?
Why plaster a crumbling wall of mud?

Hands as your Persian wheel,   2
  string your good actions,[144]
  yoke your mind to the well's depths,
draw up elixir,
  water your flowerbeds,
  you'll be the gardener's prized possession.

Lust and anger your two shovels,   3
  dig out all the weeds, my brothers.
The deeper you go,
  the more joy sprouts forth.
  The actions we do, can't be erased.

Herons can turn into swans again   4
  if you choose, compassionate One.
Slave of slaves, Nanak prays,
  be compassionate, our compassionate One.

7

In the in-laws' home, all is joint ownership,   1
  here in the natal home I see things divided.[145]
I am incompetent, why blame another?
  I just don't know how to keep things together.

My Sahiba, I'm lost in doubt.
I sing the syllables as they're written out,
  I don't know the sacred verse.[146]

2 If I wore a skirt embroidered with you all over,
  I'd be called your wife.
 If I ran my house with no taste for vice,
  I'd be my husband's beloved.

3 Pandit, if you're a learned visionary,
  from the two syllables make me two boats.[147]
 Nanak prays, may one of them carry me across,
  I want to be with truth.

8

1 Like a child, the king of a flimsy city
  falls for the bad.
 He reads he has two mothers and two fathers,[148]
  —reflect on this, dear pandit.

Master pandit, teach us, please,
how to get hold of the holder of our life-breath, Pranapati.

2 Inner fire boosts vegetation
  the ocean is bundled up together
 both moon and sun are in us
  this knowledge we do not possess.

3 Keep in mind, Ram is the all-pervasive One,
  illusion is seductive.
 Be mindful of her traits,
  hoard riches of compassion.

I live with people who won't hear what they are told   4
    nor taste what they eat.
Nanak humbly says, I am a slave of slaves,
    one instant a fraction, the next a whole.[149]

9

Forget the name, and we become crows in this world.[150]   1
Forsake the name, and we fall for the bait we see.
The mind wavers, awareness sinks.
False love for the world must break.

How heavy is the burden of toxic lust and anger?
Without the name, how can we behave virtuously?

This house of sand stands in a whirlpool,   2
this bubble is a raindrop, look
a mere drop shaped on the potter's wheel,
all light inside is the name's handmaid.

My supreme guru created everyone.   3
Devoted to your feet, we serve you,
steeped in the name, we long for you.
Hide from the name, and we leave as thieves.
We collect poisons in our scarf and lose our honor.   4
Colored by the true name, we go home in honor.
All is done by Prabhu's will,
in awe of it, mother,
    we grow fearless.

5 A wife goes for beauty and pleasure,
   her betel nuts, flowers, sugary tastes
       fester into disorders,
   the more she enjoys her games, the more she grieves.
   In the refuge of Prabh's lap, we do what we should.

6 All decked up in heavy outfits,
   her puffed-up beauty is lost,
   hopes and expectations block her door.
   Without the name,
       her home is empty, her environs vacant.

7 Turn away, daughter, my princess,
   recite the name, dress up in truth.
   Lean on Prabh's love, serve your beloved
   with the guru's sacred word,
       don't thirst for toxic stuff.

8 The charmer has charmed my mind,
   through the guru's sacred word,
       I see you.
   Thirsty Nanak stands at Prabhu's door,
   feed me your name,
       be kind to me.

10

1 A mind lost in delusions comes and goes,
   greedy, it grows greedier, lured by illusion.
   Without love for the One, it flails about
   like a fish, hooked by its neck.

The true name brings the lost mind on track.
It thinks of the guru's sacred word serenely in love.

A mind lost in delusion is a buzzing bee,   2
lured by vice, its senses are wrecked.
Like an elephant trapped in lust,
it gets tied up in chains,
        and smacked on its head.

A mind with no devotion is a silly frog.   3
Corrupt without the name,
        condemned at court,
it has no class, honor, or name.
Troubles befriend the virtueless.

A roving mind cannot hold still.   4
Not steeped in Hari's elixir,
        it lacks honor and status.
You hear us, you protect us,
all knowing, you behold the creation
        you uphold yourself.

If you lead me astray,   5
        who do I turn to?
I want to meet the guru, mother,
        to share my sorrows.
Give up vice, earn virtues,
color in the guru's sacred word,
        soak in truth.

6 Meeting the guru hones wisdom.
I-me washes out, the mind turns pure,
free forever, trapped by none,
it sings the name and nothing else.

7 This mind comes and goes at Hari's will.
The One is in us all,
        there's nothing more to say.
All go by the will, all flow into the will
all pain and joy are your will.

8 Ever attentive, you never forget us.
We grow wiser, hearing the guru's sacred word.
Our voluptuous master, the sacred word holds you,[151]
Nanak's mind enjoys praising truth.

11

1 Thirsty to see,
people steep in the One,
        keeping dualities away.
Stirring, sipping ambrosia,
        their suffering dispels.
Those facing the guru are enlightened,
        they join the One.

So many cry out, longing to see you,
so rare those who discern by joining the guru's sacred word.

2 Vedas say, speak and sing of the One,
the infinite, whose limits can't be known.

The one creator created the world,
upholds the earth and skies,
    without a thing to hold them.

The One is knowledge, meditation, melody, sacred verse,   3
yet untold is the tale of the boundless One.
The true sign is the one sacred word,
the perfect guru makes the all-knowing known.

There is only one religion,[152]   4
    but so few hold on to this truth.
The guru's insight reveals
    the absolute One across time.
Tuned in to the unstruck, absorbed in the One,
the guru-facing see the unseen infinite.

One throne, one emperor,   5
one carefree sovereign to rule over all.
The three worlds' reality is its doing,
the unfathomable, imperceptible One being.[153]

One image, truth its name,   6
where true justice is dispensed.
Those who do true actions,
win honors and celebration at the true court.

There is one devotion, there is one love.   7
Without awe or devotion, we come and go.
The guru teaches us to live here as guests,[154]
steeped in Hari's elixir, to be greeted in the hereafter.

8   In serene joy I see you all around,
except you, my master, I love no other.
Nanak: the sacred word burns off I-me,
the true guru reveals the scene of truth.

12

1   You are the bee, the flower, the vine,[155]
you the congregation, companion, communion.

A bee breathes such fragrance that
trees blossom, woods become green.

2   You are the lotus, you its lover,[156]
you revel as you proclaim your sacred word.

3   You are the calf, the cow, the rice pudding.
You are the temple, the pillar, this body.

4   You are the deed, you the doer,
you are the guru-facing, you the focus.

5   Ever creating, you watch over, creator,
your light is life to countless beings.

6   You are the deep ocean of virtue,
unborn, a pure unparalleled diamond.[157]

7   You are the creator, you the creative power,
autonomous ruler, your subjects thrive.

Hari's delicious name satisfies Nanak, 8
without beloved Hari guru, life has no taste.

PRABHATI RAGA

1

By the guru's grace, reflect on knowledge,[158] 1
    study more and more, win honors.
The light in us sparks on its own,
    the ambrosial name springs forth.[159]

Creator, you are my patron,
I ask of you one favor,
    gift me your name.

Seize the five sprinting thieves, and 2
    mental pride recedes.
Myopic sight and ignorance disappear—
    such is divine knowledge.

The alms I beg: 3
    The rice of discipline and truth
    The wheat of compassion
    The milk of action
    The butter of contentment
The food in my leaf bowl
    the One.

4 A cow bearing mercy and patience,
   I, her calf serenely suckling her milk,
   beg to be decked in your praise and beauty,
   Nanak sings rapt in Hari's song.

2

1 Mind deludes, dashes wild.[160]
   A bird, it flies across the skies.
   The sacred word catches the thief,
   the city floods in cheers.
   If you keep us, we are safe,
   our capital intact.

   The jewel of the name is my treasure.
   Give me the guru's insight,
   let me touch your feet.

2 The mind is an ascetic, a hedonist,
   the mind is a stupid boor.
   The mind is a giver, a beggar,
   the mind is the supreme guru creator.
   Mindful of the ultimate being,
   we kill the five and live in bliss.[161]

3 It is said the One exists in each heart,
   but who has seen what the lips profess?
   The fake end up upside down,[162]
   without the name, they lose respect.
   If you join us, we remain together,
   it depends on your will.

240

Do not ask about caste or clan,   4
    tell us about the true home.
What's caste, what's status?
    It's the actions we do.
Nanak: the pain of birth and death goes,
    the name sets us free.

3

Merrily wide awake, yet blindly robbed away,   1
a noose around our neck,
    yet obsessed with worldly stuff.
Expecting we come, craving we go,
tangled in this thread, we lose control.

The ever-awake One is the life of all life,
an ocean of rapture, full of ambrosial treasures.

Too deaf to hear, too blind to see,   2
    on we go with our rotten acts.
Even so, the supreme ruler Paramesaru
    gives us love, and our actions earn praise.

As each day arrives, a bit of life departs,   3
    illusion still sticks to the heart.
A speck of dualism, and we sink,
    the guru is our only refuge.

Night and day, you watch over us,   4
    you give us the joy or pain we've earned before.[163]

Bereft of merit, Nanak begs of truth,
    grant me some respect.

4

1   If I stay silent, I am called an idiot.
    If I babble, I lose out on your love.
    Our slips and flaws are judged at your court.[164]
    No morality, without your name.

    The world spins in lies,
    critics scorn me, but I am in love.

2   Those the world scorns, really know how to live,
    the guru's sacred word is their mark at court.
    That name is the first cause, they see deep inside,
    watched by the gaze of love, they know how to live.

3   I am rotten, truth is radiant,
    calling ourselves glorious won't make us so.
    The brazen self-facing eat up heavy toxins,
    but the guru-facing are absorbed in the name.

4   Blind, deaf, crazy, foolish,
    lowest of the low, wretched of the wretched,
    our only wealth
        is love for the name,
    the best wealth.
        All else is toxic ash.

Think of the sacred word, not praise or blame.   5
Greet the One who gives gifts.
You bless us with status and respect,
Nanak speaks as he is made to speak.

5

Eating more adds to waste,   1
    dressing up depletes family assets,
babbling away stirs up disputes.
    Keep in mind,
    it's all venom without the name.

Baba, my mind is stuck in such a mess,
it churns but seeks serene enlightenment.

We eat venom, we speak venom,   2
    we do venomous deeds.
Tied to death's door we get beaten,
    even so, the true name sets us free.

Just as we come, we leave,   3
    carrying our record of deeds.
The self-facing lose their capital,
    they're punished at the court.

The world is tainted, truth is pure,   4
    so we learn by the guru's sacred word.
There are few people we know,
    who know Murari deep within.

5   They bear the unbearable,
        and from their font flows beautiful bliss forever.
    Nanak, will you let me?
        As a fish loves water,
        may I love you?

6

1   Song, music, cheers, slick tricks,
    pleasures, passions, powers of all kinds,
    dressing up, fine dining,
        —nothing excites me.
    True serene bliss lies in the name.

    How would I know what you do or make me do?
    All I know is my body is soothed by the name alone.

2   Yoga, joy, delicacies, bliss,
    wisdom, truth, and love,
        —this is all Gobind's devotion.
    For my job I sing songs of praise, while
    the ruler of the sun and moon glows deep inside.[165]

3   "Love, my love," my heart
        is etched in love for my beloved,
    protector of the poor, beloved of the forests.
    By day and by night the name is my offering and fast,
    the thought of its reality stills the restless waves.

4   What strength have I to tell the untold?
    I worship you, you make me do it,

244

you live inside, the me-mine left,
I serve you, and no other.

Sweetest elixir is the guru's sacred word,   5
an ambrosia found within.
Nanak:
    those who taste it, attain the supreme state,
their thirst quenched, their body is in bliss.

NOTES TO THE TRANSLATION

Daily Worship

MORNING HYMN

1 The title of Guru Nanak's hymn is derived from *japu*, to recite repetitively. According to *Śabadārath Srī Granth Sāhibjī*, it was called *Japu* "because it was composed to be recited over and over again"—"*jo muṛa muṛa japana laī racī gaī hai*" (1969: 1). Designed for personal contemplation, this inaugural composition of the GGS is not set in the musical framework.

2 "Will," *hukamu*, is the divine order or command.

3 The "written" (*likhiā*) or "writ" (*lekhā*) or "to write" (*likhi*) is an all-embracing Nanakian principle. For more discussion, see the Introduction.

4 The original *haumai* is literally "I-me." By constantly centering on the "I," "me," and "mine," the individual is wrenched from their universal root and reduced to a narrow self-centered character.

5 "True by name" is *satu nāmu*. Truth is *the* name of the infinite One, while all other names are merely its aspects.

6 Guru Nanak categorically denounces the theory of incarnation. The One does not descend into the world in any form.

7 Some medieval yoga traditions used sound vibrations as meditational techniques for spiritual liberation, but for Guru Nanak it is the sound of sounds, prior to all sonic distinctions.

8 The Hindu gods of creation (Brahma), preservation (Vishnu), and destruction (Shiva). Gorakhu in the original is Vishnu.

9 A "guru" is not a spiritual master or a goddess or a sacred book as such, but any insight, any awakening to the universal matrix of all beings. In this volume the term "guru" is not capitalized, except when it refers to the historical Gurus.

10 Stanzas 8–11 bring up the importance of the sonic role in the awakening of the spiritual sensibility. The spiritual achievers are from diverse religious traditions. The siddhas are the eighty-four mystics believed to have attained immortality through the practice

of yoga. The *nāthas* trace their lineage to Adinath, the original master, Lord Shiva.

11   The four stanzas on "listening" are followed by four on "embracing" the wondrous name. Like many other Nanakian terms, *manne* is a multivalent term that signifies having trust or faith, remembering, accepting. In my previous works, I translated this term as "remembering" (Singh 1996: 51) and as "having faith" (2012: 38), but "embracing" seems more appropriate as it indicates a reaching out to the name and making it a part of the embodied self. Later in stanza 21 Guru Nanak expresses his triple maxim: by listening (*suṇiā*) and by embracing in the mind (*mannia manu*), we evoke love (*kītā bhāu*) for the One.

12   The unspecified "five" (*pañca*) appear frequently in Guru Nanak's compositions. Rather than the "saints" or the "elect," as usually translated, these refer to the five senses, which can be honed into five virtues: truth (*sati*), contentment (*santokhu*), morality (*dharamu*), compassion (*daiā*), and patience (*dhīraju*); or conversely, degenerate into five vices: lust (*kāma*), anger (*krodhu*), greed (*lobhu*), attachment (*mohu*), and pride (*ahaṁkāru*). Guru Nanak also refers to these latter five as "thieves" that rob humans of their authentic self.

13   "Union," *saṁjogu*, with the One.

14   In the original both terms *tanu* and *deha* denote the "body."

15   "Wealth" in the original *ātha* from *artha* (Shackle 1981: 24).

16   With slight variation, this passage forms the opening of Asa raga (GGS: 347), and also of the evening prayer, which takes its title from the beginning two words of the opening stanza (*so daru,* literally, "that gate," GGS: 8). Thus it appears three times in the GGS.

17   Instead of the usual classification scheme of musical modes into ragas and *rāginīs,* their female "consorts," here we have ragas and *parīs,* or "fairies."

18   Dharamraja, the king or judge of *dharamu* (righteousness).

19   Chitra and Gupta are the two attendants of Dharamraja; they record everybody's actions for him.

20   Indra, the king of the gods in Hindu mythology.

21   The four sources of life: egg, fetus, sweat, and earth.

22   Later in this passage it becomes clear that the author is addressing member(s) of the Aipanth; see n. 23.

23   "Mother's sect," Aipanth, one of the twelve sects of yogis who worship Ai Bhavani, a primeval mother goddess.

24 The original *bhaṁḍāraṇi* identifies the treasurer or storekeeper as female.

25 In the original *ikīsa* indicates the single (*ikku*) divine (*isu*), though *ikīsa* is also numeral 21.

26 The five are the five senses. See above n. 12.

27 A metaphor for the good and the bad.

28 Here, as in the preceding stanza, Guru Nanak uses the central pan-Indian term *dharamu*, dharma, denoting religion, virtue, duty, propriety, morality, cosmic order, and law, without the conventional fourfold class division of Indian society (Brahmans, Kshatriyas, Vaishyas, and Shudras). No action is singled out or reserved for anyone. But whatever is done has an effect. The universal injunction plays out: as you sow, so shall you reap.

29 Stanzas 34–37 depict a spiritual journey through the realms of duty (*dharamu*), knowledge (*giānu*), beauty (*saramu*), action (*karamu*), and truth (*sacu*).

30 Dhruva is the polar star.

31 The term *saramu*—designating the third realm in the "Morning Hymn"—is ambiguous. Different translators have derived it from the Sanskrit *śrama*, meaning effort; the Sanskrit *śarman*, meaning joy or bliss; or the Persian *sharm*, meaning shame, humility, surrender. McLeod presents the debate effectively and opts to translate *saramu* as "effort" (1968: 222–223). In the same vein, Talib chooses "spiritual endeavor" (1984: 21), while Gopal Singh uses the Persian "surrender" (1978: 11). Macauliffe in his notes firmly states, "*Sharm* here is not the Persian *sharm*, shame nor the Sanskrit *sharam*, toil. It is the Sanskrit *sharman*, happiness" (1909: 216). I rely on the "Morning Hymn" own gloss of *saramu* as *rūpu*, "beauty" or "form" (*saramu khaṇḍu kī bāṇī rūpu*—"the realm of *saramu* is beauty itself").

32 "Sharpen" (*ghaṛīai*) means to file a blunt thing like a pencil or a blade.

33 Exegetes and translators have also contested the meaning of *karamu* designating the fourth "Morning Hymn" realm. For a full discussion, see McLeod (1968: 223) and N. G. K. Singh (1993: 86–88). I find "action" an appropriate designation for a realm that is "full of force" and consists of active agents, the "mighty warriors and heroes."

34 Guru Nanak here depicts Sita, the ancient Indian paradigm of female power, in the plural: "*sīto sītā.*" However, translators

and exegetes of the "Morning Hymn" have responded differently to Guru Nanak's reference. For further discussion, see N. G. K. Singh 2007: 38–42.

35   The realm of truth is the fifth and final stage of the spiritual journey. The individual comes face to face with infinity itself and partakes of the qualities of the true One.

36   In this final stanza, the fivefold spiritual journey is embodied in the goldsmith artistically designing the sacred word on the crucible of love in his smithy, while vigorously engaged in his everyday social and economic affairs. For an analysis of this passage, see N. G. K. Singh (2017: 113–134).

37   The term "awe" I suggest is a better translation of *bhau* than ordinary "fear." Rudolph Otto's familiar phrase *mysterium tremendum et fascinans* perfectly captures Guru Nanak's analogy. In order to produce fresh designs, the goldsmith must ignite the creative fire with the bellows of awe.

38   "Love" in the original is *bhāu* with a long -*ā*-, whereas "awe" (see previous note) is *bhau* with a short -*a*-. The integral relationship between the emotions of awe (*bhau*) and love (*bhāu*) is constant in Guru Nanak's oeuvre.

39   This concluding lyric (*saloku*) is recited several times during the day by the devout. A slightly different version by the second Guru is on p. 146 of the GGS, with minor changes.

EVENING HYMNS
That Gate

40   The evening recitation takes the title from the opening words "*So daru*" (That gate). This is a collection of nine hymns by different authors, in different ragas and of varying length (GGS: 8–12). The first five are clustered under "That Gate," and the latter four under "That Purakhu." Every hymn carries the name of the raga it is sung to (in this instance Asa), followed by the term *mahalā* ("palace," here "section") and a number identifying the Guru who composed it (*mahalā* 1 for Guru Nanak; *mahalā* 2 for the second Guru, Angad, and so on).

41   The recitation opens with stanza 27 of the "Morning Hymn," only in the evening version there are more second-person pronouns like "yours" (*tera*) and "you" (*tudhno*).

42   "Toll-free," without any obstructions. I am grateful to Orsini: her suggestion "tolls" for the original "*ṭhāki*" brings out Guru Nanak's

usage of concrete worldly metaphors to convey metaphysical messages.

43 "Daily practice" in the original is *raharāsi;* it is now the name of the evening prayer.

44 "Descendant of Madhu" in the original is *mādhojī* (from Sanskrit Mādhava), an epithet for Krishna. Used by Guru Nanak for the non-incarnate divine.

That Purakhu

45 Here begins the second segment of four hymns called "That Purakhu," in Asa raga; the first three are marked *mahalā* 4 (by Guru Ram Das), the fourth is *mahalā* 5 (by Guru Arjan).

46 The suffix *jī* for respect and intimacy is retained in this hymn, so "*tudhujī*" literally means "you my friend."

47 The "six" (*khaṭu*) actions are not identified. Sahib Singh (1962, GGS: 11) thinks that this a reference to the six Brahmanical duties mentioned in the *Laws of Manu.* These would be the six duties mentioned in Book 10: teaching, studying, sacrificing for himself, sacrificing for others, giving gifts, and receiving gifts (Manu 10:74–75); or the six from Book 12: studying the Veda, performing austerities, gaining knowledge, subjugating the organs, abstaining from inflicting injury, and serving the guru (Manu 12:83).

48 "True" (*satī* in the original) evokes the devotion of women who cremated themselves on the funeral pyre of their husband.

LATE EVENING HYMN
Praise

49 "Praise" is the late evening prayer, recited just before going to bed (GGS: 12–13). For its ceremonial performance, see Introduction. It includes hymns in Asa raga, Dhanasari raga, and Gauri raga, which is the most popular raga in the GGS (GGS: 151–346). As we notice here and later in section 5, this raga appears in a number of variants (Gauri Dipaki, Gauri Purabi, Gauri Guareri, and so on).

50 A poignant allegory for death. A newlywed is welcomed in the groom's home by the festive pouring of oil on its threshold, and oil is also poured to light up the crematory fire.

51 Refers to the custom of including a brightly colored thread with an auspicious invitation.

52 Refers to the six Indian philosophical systems: Samkhya, Yoga, Nyaya, Vaisheshika, Mimamsa, and Vedanta.

53 "*Bābā*" is an endearing term for an older man. Guru Nanak himself is often called Baba Nanak in the *Janamsākhīs* (see Introduction).

54 The passage rings audibly with Guru Nanak's respect for the diversity of teachers and schools of thought.

55 Waving a whisk is a way of showing respect to an honored guest.

56 The hymn is set in the *Pūrabī* ("eastern") style of Gauri raga.

57 "Circle of circles" in the original, "*maṇḍalu maṇḍā.*"

58 "Self-seekers," *sākatu* (from *śākta*, or worshipers of *śakti*, or divine power) is used loosely by Guru Nanak for swindlers who use yogic powers for self-promotion; preoccupied with themselves, they are not interested in the divine. For further information on these "opponent others" in bhakti rhetoric, see Pauwels 2010: 509–539.

59 The wish to be the "dust of feet" is a cultural expression for humility and devotion.

Ballad in the Melody of Hope

1 This heading for the composition indicates that it be sung in the tune of the popular ballad of the maimed King As. Guru Nanak's "Ballad in the Melody of Hope" (*Āsā dī vār*) includes lyrics by himself and by his immediate successor, Guru Angad (indicated respectively in the GGS with *mahalā* 1 and *mahala* 2, or M1 and M2 for short).

2 This ballad (*vār*) is structured in twenty-four segments. Each segment starts with "lyrics" (*saloku*) by the first and second gurus and concludes with a key verse, called *pauṛī* (step), which I have translated as "envoi."

3 "Mark," in the original *nīsāṇu*, is used frequently by Guru Nanak and means sign, mark, stamp, distinction.

4 *Kudarati* (Ar. *qudrat*) in the original, meaning "nature," "power," "might," identifies creation with the creative power, the visible multiverse with its internal divine force and dynamism.

5 The name written "within" (*andar*) each being (*Śabadārath Sri Guru Granth Sāhibjī* 1969: vol. 1, 463) governs individual morality (*dharamu*).

6 Again, the original term is *kudarati*.

7 This simile first appears in the "Morning Hymn," stanza 37.

8 Once again, Guru Nanak is playing on awe (*bhau*) and love (*bhāu*): the power and magnificence of the One evoke love. See n. 38 in section 1.

9   Guru Nanak expresses his praise for Muslims using Persian words: a slave (*bandā*) who is totally in submission/captivity (*bandī*) to behold God. He celebrates the Islamic ideal of submission to God. Elsewhere he uses the Sanskrit *dāsu*.

10 In the original *satī* could refer to widows, who are content, committed to sacrificing themselves.

11 An alternative reading of this verse, "you care for them all too."

12 An expression of humility.

13 The passage evokes both Muslim burial and Hindu cremation rites.

14 The true guru is the sacred word, the medium of revelation. Thus the medium (true guru) and the message (the One/*ikk*) are the same.

15 The self is an agent—through knowledge we can shift our praxis. This extends Guru Nanak's thought in the preceding lyric: only by recognizing our ego do we become cognizant of the divine door.

16 "Yoga of serenity" (*sahaj*) is idealized by Guru Nanak as serene consciousness, in harmony with the universal One. Rather than as a specific technique of meditation, Guru Nanak uses *sahaj* loosely to express the ultimate state of serenity achieved naturally and spontaneously.

17 Guru Nanak identifies himself as "a low-caste songster" (*hau ḍhāḍī kā nīcu jāti*).

18 "Hold truth in the scarf" (*pallai hoe*). People tie the edge of their scarves or shawls in knots, using them as purses.

19 "Off the saints' feet," from the opening line.

20 Before dyeing, fabric is steeped in a solution of alum (*pāhu*). Guru Nanak utilizes this essential chemical ingredient for the divine One.

21 *Khumbi caṛhāi*, copper over which fabric is steam cleaned. This chemical process is reminiscent of the smithy scene from stanza 38 of the "Morning Hymn."

22 "Birth" here refers to caste (*jāti*). Alternative translations interpret *jāti* as creation, but Guru Nanak is playing on the words *jāti* (caste), *joti* (light), and *jātā* (known). He emphasizes that the divine light (*joti*) is in each caste (*jāti*), and that is how everyone is known (*jātā*), that is their identity.

23 "Very self," *ātamu* (Skt. *ātman*), the individual, microcosmic self.

24 "Peak" for the original *meru* may refer to the mythical Meru mountain or the primary bead in a rosary.

25 In this stanza Guru Nanak refers to the four Yugas of Hindu

cosmology to show the steady decline from the age of perfection to the present. He mentions the Satya Yuga (golden age), Treta Yuga (silver age), Dvapara Yuga (bronze age), and the present dark age of Kali Yuga. The four Yugas follow one another. In this sequence human physique and morality suffer severe decline.

26   In this stanza, Guru Nanak's sequence of *Sama Veda*, *Ṛg Veda*, *Yajur Veda*, and *Atharva Veda* does not follow the chronological order of the traditional four Vedas, nor does it make specific textual references to the four. The four Vedas represent an all-embracing body of knowledge that comes out true for people across the four ages who read, recite, and reflect. Guru Nanak purposefully transcends religious boundaries "Hindu," "Jain," and "Muslim" by addressing the same divine One across time and space through a rich plurality of names. Alliterative sound seems to govern his choice: in the *Sama Veda* the divine One is named Svetambara, the white-clad Jain guide; in the *Ṛg Veda* it is called Ram; in the *Yajur Veda* its name is Krishna the Yadav; and in the *Atharva Veda* it is called the Islamic Allah.

27   A milkmaid (*gopī*), rival of Radha's. The story of Chandravali does not appear in the actual texts of the *Yajur Veda* itself.

28   This coral tree (*Erythrina indica*) is a mythical tree in Indra's heaven, brought by Krishna to Dwarka.

29   Reference to Babur's invasion of India.

30   Reference to the Gayatri mantra, the most sacred verse in the *Ṛg Veda* (3.62.10).

31   In Sikh memory, Nanak spoke these words as a nine-year-old boy during his Upanayana ceremony, the critical Hindu rite of passage when the young "twice-born" boy is given the sacred thread (*janeu*) and the Gayatri mantra. Spurning the ritual thread to be worn externally, Nanak asks the Brahman, the master of ceremonies, for an interior thread emotionally and spiritually woven with a "twist of truth" (*satu vaṭu*). For more on this popular narrative, see N. G. K. Singh 2005: 78–81. In the next few stanzas of his hymn, Guru Nanak harshly rejects the ritual sanctification of caste hierarchies and gender exclusivism that is spun into the thread worn on the body. (For a detailed study of caste and sex differences and hierarchies reinforced by the Upanayana rite of passage, see B. Smith 1986: 73.)

32   This stanza depicts the contrast between the covert profane actions people tend to do on a daily basis and the overt sacred customs they

lavishly celebrate. In the wearing of the sacred thread, Upanayana ritual is conducted by the Brahman priest and attended by family members and friends. See n. 31 above.

33 The Brahman honored for conducting special rituals is put to shame for his routinized acts.

34 An acerbic critique of the Brahman who invests others with the sacred thread, a sign of purity and truth. The places he visits are immoral; what he does, speaks, and sees is immoral. His feet, hands, tongue, and eyes do not wear the thread with the "twist of truth."

35 Guru Nanak views the Brahman as "the ignorant one," lit. "mentally blind" (*mani andhā*). He is disappointed that society reveres Brahmans as "wise" (*sujāṇu*).

36 The verse addresses the hypocritical behavior of Brahmans who collaborate with the Muslim rulers: they levy taxes on their fellow Brahmans and their cattle, but use dung from the same cattle to purify their own kitchen floor.

37 "Foreigners" (*mleccha* in the original) who do not belong to the Brahmanical *varṇa* (class) order. In this context it refers to the Mughal rulers and their officers.

38 An allusion to the establishment of the new Mughal regime.

39 "Ahead" (*aggai*) implies the hereafter.

40 The original *siranhāvaṇī* (head washing) is a euphemism for a woman's period, when she was required to wash her hair.

41 An expression for all material and spiritual wealth.

42 The word "priest" is implied.

43 A popularly cited passage for the equality of women.

44 This recalls the image in stanza 34 of the "Morning Hymn."

45 "Corrected" (*sudhu*) indicates that the text had been corrected by the editor, in this instance, Guru Arjan (*mahalā* 5).

Discourse with the Siddhas

1 Here Guru Nanak enters an enclave of siddhas. This dialogue with the siddhas (*Siddha gosṭi*) in seventy-three stanzas is set in Ramkali raga (GGS: 938–946). The speakers in the dialogue are not identified.

2 Some commentators attribute this verse to the yogis, I follow Sahib Singh in attributing it to Guru Nanak: "This is Guru Nanak Dev Ji's response" (Sahib Singh 1962: 938).

3 A name for Vishnu, here used for the non-incarnate divine.

4   Charpat (11th-12th century) is revered as an immortal Nath, a disciple of Gorakh, the celebrated founder of the Nath order. "Renunciate" in the original is *audhū* (from *avadhūtā*), literally one who has shaken off the world.

5   These are the clothes and accessories of the Gorakhnathi sect of yogis.

6   *Khatu darśan* in the original for the six philosophical systems of Nyaya, Vaisheshika, Samkhya, Yoga, Mimamsa, and Vedanta.

7   Large earrings were worn by *kanphaṭ* ("ear-split") ascetics as markers of spiritual knowledge.

8   Along with air, water, fire, and earth, the fifth element is ether.

9   The "serpent of illusion," *māyā*.

10   The Buddhist term *sunnu* (Skt. *śūnya*) is used here for the divine without any attributes.

11   "Traveling ascetic" in the original is *udāsī*. Guru Nanak's four prolonged travels are called *udāsīs*. "Udasi" is also the name of an ascetic group claiming descent from Siri Chand, one of Guru Nanak's two sons.

12   A reference to the cycle of reincarnation.

13   The unstruck (*anahati/anahadu*) sound with no beginning and no end is heard at the finale of the yogic process.

14   "Three strands," *traiguṇa*, are truth (*sattva*), passion (*rajas*), inertia (*tamas*), on which matter and creation are woven. "Chew on iron" means to do the impossible.

15   "Real," *akalapatu*, "uncontrived, uninvented" (Shackle 1981: 10, from Skt. *akalpita*).

16   "Sharpen," *ghaṛīai*, also used in "Morning Hymn." stanza 36.

17   *Paracā* (relish or delight) is used in several expressions with different connotations: take delight in, become familiar with, get to know (*Mahān Koś* 1960: 558); "trust" (*Śabadārath* 1969: vol. 3, 840, *bharosā*). Shackle (1981: 182, under *paracā*) interprets it as "mystical experience."

18   "Know" is implied.

19   The eight *siddhi* miraculous powers include the power to make one's body smaller than the smallest (*aṇimā*), greater than the greatest (*mahimā*), lighter than the lightest (*laghimā*), heavier than the heaviest (*garimā*); the power to acquire everything (*prāpti*); the power to experience every joy (*prakāmya*); superiority over all (*īśitvā*); and mastery over the self (*vaśitvā*). See Phillips 2009: 247.

20 The meaning of *sara apasara* (translated here as "good ways and bad") is unclear.

21 Ten *sannyasi* orders, divided into six and four, are said to have been established by Śaṅkara. For details, see Nayar and Sandhu 2007: 164.

22 "Here and there" implies this world and the next.

23 Those facing the guru (*gurumukhi*) are compared with the heroic Ram and his virtuous allies, who built a bridge of stones connecting South India to Lanka in order to free Sita.

24 Babhikhan (Skt. Vibhishana) was Ravana's virtuous brother, who joined god Ram and helped defeat the demon Ravana.

25 Thirty-three crore (330,000,000) indicates the multitudes that the guru-centered can rescue.

26 *Pavanu* (air) here means the air we breathe, "breath."

27 Love is usually hot, but for the Guru it brings in serene joy that gets rid of all anxiety.

28 "Shade," *chāiā*, implies protection. According to Sikh exegetes the coolness of the moon and the heat of the sun refer to opposite mental energies in the yogic system, cool mind and hot knowledge (Sahib Singh 1962: 943).

29 The meaning "mind" is implied by the original *sasi* (moon).

30 "Real merges into real," *tato tatu*, "reality into reality."

31 The "fourth" state is that of ultimate unity.

32 In yogic physiognomy, the nine natural openings of the body allow the experience of the physical world, and the tenth door opens at the finale of the yogic process.

33 The "distance of the three and seven fingers" refers to the inner heart from the navel in yogic terminology. Nayar and Sandhu 2007: 165.

34 "Word guru," *sabadu guru*.

35 Ten fingers is the distance at which the breath will just move a fine piece of cotton wool. For an explanation, see Dass 2008: 184.

36 "The three yogic channels," *suṣumnā, iḍā, piṅgala*.

37 "Inner self," *ātamu*.

38 In Guru Nanak's poetics the "elephant mind" is ignorantly intoxicated (GGS: 351), egotistically inflated (GGS: 1286), trapped in lust (GGS: 1188); the opposite of a mind drunk on the wondrous One.

39 Allusion to the yogic process of sun entering the house of moon, from the preceding line.

40 In yoga practice the navel is the center of breathing.

41 "Unborn" literally, with no family; "*akulīṇu*" in the original.

42 This final stanza of the "Discourse with the Siddhas" (73) addresses the divine one directly, and so in its literary format, it differs from the rest of the composition. It is missing in the "Discourse with the Siddhas" recorded in the collection prepared under the auspices of Nanak 3, and textual scholars speculate that it was added by Guru Arjan during his compilation of the GGS (P. Singh 2000: 102).

Thematic Compositions
THE HOURS

1 "The Hours" composition is set in Sirirag raga (GGS: 74–75) and is the first in the genre of four "The Hours" hymns (the third is by Guru Ram Das, and the fourth by Guru Arjan).

2 "Quarter," *paharu*, about a three-hour period; "roving" for *vañajāriā*, a nomadic trader.

3 An allusion to humans free of all caste and class obligations.

4 "Name," *nāmu*, the name for the One. For more, see Introduction.

THE DAYS OF THE LUNAR MONTH

5 The poetic form of this composition is based on the monthly cycle of the lunar days, *thitī*, the "dates." It is set in Bilaval raga (GGS: 838–840).

6 "Egg" (*aṇḍaja*) is variously interpreted: some scholars think Guru Nanak is talking of a cosmic egg, but usually *aṇḍaja* in his verse refers to one of the four sources of life: egg, fetus, earth, and sweat ("Ballad in the Melody of Hope," stanza 8; GGS: 467). He frequently uses the numeral "four" to represent the four sources as in stanza 5 of this composition (see n. 7 below).

7 The "four" sources are egg, fetus, earth, and sweat.

8 The eighteen Puranas.

9 "Six" short for the six philosophical systems (*darśana*): Samkhya, Yoga, Nyaya, Vaisheshika, Mimamsa, and Vedanta; "three," the three strands (*guṇas*) on which matter and creation are woven: *sattva, rajas,* and *tamas*—truth, passion, inertia.

10 "Fourth stage," "*turīā*" (Skt. *turīya*), the consciousness of totality. This fourth state is beyond the three: awake state, semiconscious dream state, and the unconsciousness of deep sleep.

11 The five senses, which in this instance have degenerated into lust, anger, greed, attachment, and pride. See section 1, n. 12.

12 Here the "six" are explicitly stated as "philosophies" (*darśana*). See above n. 9.

13 "Unstruck," *anhadu.*

14 Taran Singh (1969: 855), *Mahān Koś* (1960: 136), the authors of the Faridkot commentary (1970: 1728) and the *Śabadārath* (1969: vol. 3, 839) interpret "seven" as the five senses, plus mind and consciousness.

15 Reference to the traditional eight *siddhi* powers. See Glossary, number 8 (also section 3, n. 19).

16 "Masters," *nātha.*

17 According to Taran Singh, "mother here means Hari himself" (1969: 857). Since the verse commences with a yogi reference (the nine masters, or *nātha*), it is possible Guru Nanak meant Ai Bhavani, a primeval mother goddess (also mentioned in "Morning Hymn," stanza 28). However, Gopal Singh (1978: 797) insists that it not be "confused with the Ayee order of the yogis."

18 Cardinal practices of the Sikh faith are name (*nāmu*), which is a cognitive recollection of the singular divine; philanthropy (*dānu*) is doing good deeds for fellow beings; bathing (*isnānu*) is a means of cultivating the personal self (bathing is not a ritual at any sacred site, but a daily hygienic practice).

19 The *ekadasī* fast, observed on the eleventh day of a fortnight. Many Hindus and Jains observe it by not eating beans and grains. For certain *ekadasī* fasts over the course of the year, devotees avoid taking all food and water (Melton 2011: 647).

20 As Guru Nanak says, the true self of the person is not dependent on any food, therefore it is pointless to keep fasts.

21 "Renunciate," *audhūtā,* one who has shaken off the world.

22 "Delighted," *parcai,* is defined as "mystical awareness" (Shackle 1981: 182, *paracā*). Gopal Singh translates it as "faith" (1978: 798). For more, see section 3, n. 17.

23 Vertical *sikhar* ("peak") and horizontal *tāre* ("crosses over") motion fuse in Guru Nanak's image.

SONG OF THE TWELVE MONTHS

24 Composed in the *bārah māha* genre in Tukhari raga (GGS: 1107–1110).

25 "Ram her very being" (*ātama rāmā* in the original), which literally means "Ram is my *ātama*" (Upanishadic *ātman*).

26 The *babīhā* bird is a hawk cuckoo (also called *cātrik* or *sārang*),

believed to stay thirsty until she gets her raindrop from the clouds. Her repeated cry for the raindrop is a symbolical expression for the aching human heart in Guru Nanak's poetry. *Koel,* the Indian cuckoo, is idealized for her singing from the mango groves.

27 Chet (*caitra,* mid-March to mid-April) is the first month on the typical Indian calendar.

28 Bar is a region of the Panjab, between the rivers Beas and Ravi.

29 Cowrie shells were used as currency along trade routes in Africa, South Asia, and East Asia.

30 "Water crossings," *tīrathu.*

31 Ritual bathing at the sacred confluence of the rivers Ganga, Jamuna, and the mythic Sarasvati at Prayag (Allahabad) is considered highly meritorious in the Indian world.

32 Phalguna (mid-February to mid-March) is the last month on the Indian calendar.

SONGS OF MOURNING

33 There are five songs of mourning by Guru Nanak in Vadahans raga (GGS: 578–582). This composition is the second in the sequence.

34 Good actions are recorded in the divine court.

VERSES ON EMPEROR BABUR

35 This first Babur hymn (GGS: 360) is in Asa raga, as are the next two. Its identification 3:5:39 tells us the hymn is in 3 stanzas, 5th in the sixth *gharu* of Asa raga, and 39th in the sequence of Guru Nanak's hymns. For *gharu,* see Glossary. The term "Hindustan" is derived from *Sindhu,* the Sanskrit name for the Indus River.

36 A reference to Babur.

37 In the original *khasamu* means husband or master.

38 Though this composition and the following in the sequence are a part of the "eight-stanza" cluster in Asa raga, they actually have only seven stanzas.

39 Vermilion in the parting of a woman's hair symbolizes her married status, and that her husband is alive.

40 Jars of water for fertility and fans are typical of the joyful South Asian wedding ceremonies that greet the newlywed couple.

41 Symbolic of prosperity, love, and unity, coins are showered during a post-wedding ceremony.

42 "Time" (*vakhatu* in the original) alludes to the five daily prayers of the Muslims.

43 "Worship" (*pūjā*) indicates the Hindu mode of worship.

44 At this moment of devastation, it is too late for them to return to their Hindu tradition or turn to Islam.

45 "Woodwinds," *shehnai*, played during Indian weddings.

46 Guru Nanak reminds us that the Muslim Babur killed the Lodi rulers of Hindustan, who were likewise Muslim. Thus he offers an important insight: it is not religion but wealth and power that divide people, brother from brother.

47 Reference to Babur.

48 "By writing spells on slips of paper" (*paracā*, Shackle 1981: 182).

49 The Lodi Sultans were Pathans (Pashtuns) from Afghanistan, who spoke the Pashto language.

50 "Turk" was a standard term for "Muslim" in medieval India. "Bhatt" and "Thakur" are different social classes. Guru Nanak empathizes with women from different religious and social backgrounds who suffered alike during the Mughal invasion.

51 A reference to Muslim women, who wear the veil.

52 Reference to Hindu wives, immolating themselves.

53 This hymn (GGS: 722–723) is in Tilang raga. Its identifier 2:3:5 tells us it is in 2 stanzas, 3rd in the third *gharu* of Tilang raga, and 5th in the sequence.

54 According to the *Bālā Janamsākhī* tradition, Bhai Lalo was a carpenter by profession who lived in Saidpur (in present-day Pakistan). He served Guru Nanak with great devotion when the Guru stayed with him during his travels in that region.

55 Guru Nanak bitterly twists the metaphor of a wedding procession to describe Babur's invasion of India. This "wedding" destroyed the Muslim Lodi Sultans, along with the Hindu and Muslim masses, and set up the foundation for the Mughal Empire. Babur in his autobiography recounts his procession of warriors coming down from Afghanistan in a weddinglike festive mood as well (Thackston 1996: 310–312, 324).

56 Two terms for blood, "*khūnu*" (from Persian) and "*rakatu*" (from Sanskrit), are ironically used for the display of the auspicious saffron.

57 "City of the dead" in the original is *māsa purī*, literally city (*purī*) of meat (*māsa*), in this instance, corpses.

58 "Colorful games" by the One who creates is *rang* (color, pleasure) *ravai* ("cause to dwell," Shackle 1981: 252). Scholars have translated these words in various ways: "Yokes all to His love" (Gopal

Singh 1978: 692), "in manifold pleasures engaged it" (Talib 1984: 1503), and Sahib Singh explains (1962: GGS, 723) "attached the mortals to pleasure."

59 The numbers seventy-eight and ninety-seven refer to the years 1578 V.S. and 1597 V.S. of the Indian calendar, which correspond respectively with the years 1521 C.E. and 1540 C.E. (H. Singh, *Encyclopedia of Sikhism* 1992: 241). In 1578 V.S. (1521 C.E.) the first Mughal Emperor Babur started his invasion of India. The "disciple of humanity" (*marad kā celā*) is most likely the humane and tolerant Afghani ruler Sher Shah Suri (Taran Singh 1969: 764; Gopal Singh 1978: 692). Other scholars interpret it differently: as "warrior" (*sūrmā*, Sahib Singh 1962: GGS, 723) or as "Guru Gobind Singh's Khalsa" (Faridkot commentary, 1970: 1494). In 1597 V.S. (1540 C.E.) Sher Shah Suri drove the second Mughal Emperor, Humayun, out of India. Guru Nanak himself expired in 1539, but he had probably heard about Humayun's earlier defeat at Chausa and predicted his later expulsion. The dates 1578 V.S. and 1597 V.S. therefore refer to the beginning and (temporary) ending of the Mughal rule.

ALPHABET ON THE WOODEN BOARD

60 "Alphabet on the Wooden Board" is set in Asa raga, GGS: 432–434. A flat "wooden board" (*paṭī* in the original) used by children till recent times. It was coated with clay that would be refreshed daily for writing. The poem in thirty-five stanzas introduces letters of the Gurmukhi alphabet. Starting with "C" (stanza 9) through "Ṛ" (stanza 33) the acrostic maintains the order of the Panjabi alphabet current today, but the first eight letters and the last two are out of sequence. The poem begins with the letter "S" (fourth letter in the alphabet) and ends with "A" (second in the alphabet).

61 *Lekhā*, the written account given at death. For more, see Introduction.

62 Indicates old age.

63 The opening of the verse "*goi gāi jini choḍī galī*" is obscure, and the suggested meaning, "cowherd," is uncertain.

64 See n. 6 and n. 7 on pp. 536-537.

65 *Bhogī*, who enjoys all beings—born of egg, egg, fetus, earth, or sweat; antithesis of the ascetic yogi.

66 The traditional belief that we go through 840,000 forms of existence, among which human life is the most important.

67 Board game with a cross-shaped design; the four arms are compared with the four ages. A painting from Basohli, Jammu (1694–95), which shows Shiva and Parvati playing the *caupari* game, is displayed at the Metropolitan Museum of Art in New York.

68 Madhusudan, "killer of Madhu," epithet for Vishnu.

69 Letter "m" for *maranu* (death).

70 The names Vasudeva (indwelling god) and Paramesaru (supreme ruler) express the immanence and transcendence of the One.

71 Guru Nanak identifies himself as a poet (*sāiru*), from the Arabic word for poetry (*al-shi'r*).

THE GRACELESS

72 "Graceless," *Kucajī*. The composition is set in Suhi raga, GGS: 762.

73 The word in the original is *jīo*, lit. "life" and the suffix used for respect, here translated as "friend."

74 "Herons" symbolize the white hair of old age.

75 The "in-laws' home" is the other world.

THE GRACEFUL

76 "Graceful," *Sucajī*. This composition is also set in Suhi raga, GGS: 762.

Selections Across Musical Modes
SIRIRAG RAGA

1 "Illusion" in the original is *māyā*, which represents the false qualities of the world—its seeming permanence and durability.

2 Implies life on earth ("here") and beyond death ("there").

3 "Blessing," *bakhsīs*.

4 In the original "*daru*" can mean divine court or divine door, threshold.

5 Keeping with his Sufi symbolism, Guru Nanak uses the term *dargah* (Sufi shrine).

6 Here Guru Nanak utilizes the complex Sufi metaphor of wine. Sufi mystics frequently describe spiritual love as wine, and intoxication as the loss of the egoist self in that love. For Guru Nanak, the subtle alchemical process happens with the ingredient of the true name.

7 Going around one's beloved is a Panjabi expression for joy.

8 Reference to the divine court.

9   Rather than being anointed externally with the mark of honor on the forehead, the implication is that truth radiates naturally on the faces of those who live truthfully.

10   In contrast to the *suhāgaṇi* (the happy wife) who revels with her husband.

11   Holy Qur'an in the original is Kateb (see Glossary).

12   Eight-stanza compositions (*ashṭpadī*) in Sirirag raga begin on p. 53 of the GGS, though this hymn has only seven stanzas.

13   The word "martyr" appears in both the singular *shahīd* and the plural *suhade*.

14   Again the word *shaikh* appears both in the singular and in the plural (*masāikhu, mashaikh*).

15   *Durūd* blessings are recited for the Prophet Muhammad.

16   This line has been variously translated: "If the Lord blesses one caste, the other caste likes it not" (Gopal Singh 1978: 51); "God approves not the distinction of high caste and low caste—None has He made higher than others" (Talib 1984: 113); "one class of people does not like the other, when one has been made great " (www.srigranth.org). I simply followed the literal meaning of the verse: "Among castes you prefer no caste (*varanā varana na bhāvanī*), even if you make some higher (*je kisai vaḍā karei*)."

17   *Casā* in the original is a very short unit of time, less than 48 seconds.

18   "Blushing woman," *lālī* in the original, carries the power of blood and energy.

19   The "tenth door" is the finale of the yogic process, an opening in the body that leads to the state of liberation.

· 20   GGS: 62.

21   This verse reflects the "Morning Hymn" maxim: more important than the concept of truth is the practice of truth.

22   *Kingurī*, a stringed musical instrument connecting two gourds, plays the sacred word in each heart.

GAURI RAGA

23   Gauri raga (GGS: 151–346) is an evening melody, which is synthesized with other regional tunes and notes by Guru Nanak and his successors, so it appears in various musical styles in the GGS. Some evening liturgical hymns (section 1) are set in this raga.

24   Familial relationships are taken seriously, as each is invested with psychological and spiritual significance.

25   The identifier 4:1:18 tells us the hymn is in 4 stanzas, 1st in the

Bairāgan ("yearning") melody of Gauri raga, and 18th in the sequence (GGS: 156).

26 Cowrie: shell.

27 In earlier times the wealthy buried gold and coins underground.

28 Original *banajārani,* a female trader, free-spirited gypsy.

29 In this hymn, also in Gauri Bairagan raga, Guru Nanak idealizes females from various species for their passion.

30 This hymn has 8 stanzas and is 10th in sequence (GGS: 225).

31 Reference to the traditional sixteen articles for female decoration.

32 Although it is included among the eight-stanza cluster of Gauri raga hymns, this hymn (GGS: 229) has 9 stanzas, is 2nd in the Guareri style of Gauri raga, and 18th in the sequence.

33 Because of their material possessions, the spiritually dead are considered successful, so they are envied rather than mourned.

ASA RAGA

34 Asa raga (GGS: 347–488), the "Ballad in the Melody of Hope," begins with a slightly modified stanza 27 from "Morning Hymn." A wide range of Guru Nanak's hymns are found in this musical measure. Besides several evening hymns, his "Ballad in the Melody of Hope" (section 2), his acrostic "Alphabet on the Wooden Board," as well as three Babur compositions (section 4) are set in Asa.

35 An accomplished sage, Narada was the messenger of the gods, a heavenly musician, and a patron of singers.

36 Actions, good or bad, are all dictated by the divine will.

37 "Guests," *mahimānu.* We must appreciate this life as temporary guests, keeping our universal, infinite host ever in mind.

38 Lit. "There is no duality" (*dūjā*).

39 These five-stanza hymns in Asa raga begin on p. 354 of the GGS.

40 "Sacred thread," *janeu,* worn as a mark of the "twice-born" Hindu males. It is given to the three upper-caste boys during their respective initiation rite, and is worn throughout their life.

41 Reference to the ring made of the sacred *kuśa* grass worn on the little finger for ritual performance. The backdrop again is the Hindu initiation ceremony for the twice-born males (*upanayāna*).

42 In the original *tikkā,* the holy dot on the forehead.

43 Images the divine as "watchman" (*pāharūāru*).

44 Reference to the eighteen Puranas and to the four Vedas.

45 The "guru-facing," *gurmukhi.*

46 The 4:2:32 identification tells us it is a 4-stanza hymn, 2nd in the third *gharu* style of Asa raga, and 32nd in the sequence (GGS: 358).

47 Rice balls (*piṇḍu*) offered during funeral rites to appease the deceased are changed into the image of the "long haired" (Keshav) Krishna. According to Stoler Miller, the name Keshav is related to Krishna's killing of the horse demon Keśin (1977: 20).

48 The river Ganges and the city of Varanasi (Benares or Kashi) deemed holy in the Indic world.

49 The 4:1:35 identifier tells us this has 4 stanzas, is the 1st set in the sixth *gharu* musical style of Asa raga, and 35th in the sequence (GGS: 359).

50 Name for Krishna. Mother Yashoda ties Krishna several times as punishment for his pranks. Damodar means restrained (*dama*) at the waist or stomach (*udara*).

51 These sestets in Asa raga begin on p. 435 of the GGS.

52 Several lines in these sestets end with Ram, a pious acclamation by the poet. It is not an invocation to Ram but just an interjection at the end of the line.

53 "Seven" refer to the five senses, plus mind and consciousness.

54 "Ecstatic," *bairāgaī* (Skt: *vairāga*), means beyond the world, beyond themselves. The term appears twice in this stanza.

55 "Virtues" implied. According to Taran Singh (1969: 533) the "five" denote truth (*satu*), contentment (*santokhu*), compassion (*daiā*), righteousness (*dharamu*), and patience (*dhīraju*).

GUJARI RAGA

56 Gujari raga (GGS: 489–526) is a morning melody that opens with the hymn translated here. Very few hymns of Guru Nanak appear in this raga.

VADAHANS RAGA

57 In Vadahans raga (GGS: 557–594) we find works of Sikh Gurus patterned on Panjabi folk songs typically sung during wedding and death ceremonies. This is GGS: 557. Guru Nanak's "Songs of Mourning" (*alāhṇīāṅ*, section 4) are also set in Vadahans.

58 *Ruṇ jhuṇ* is how Guru Nanak hears the melodious call of the peacocks. The various species resonate with and echo the timeless soundless sound.

59 For "mother" Guru Nanak here uses the rare term *ammālī* (variation of *ambā*).

60 Vermilion is *sindhūr,* the auspicious red powder applied by married Hindu women in the parting of their hair. Widows can no longer wear it.

61 "Dualized body," *tanu kā birhā,* the cause of her pain and separation.

62 This hymn is identified as 1:3, 1st in the second *gharu* style of Vadahans raga and 3rd in the sequence.

63 This sestet begins GGS: 565.

64 For details on "written," see Introduction.

SORATH RAGA

65 In keeping with the light mood of Sorath raga (GGS: 595–659), Guru Nanak's hymns have a quick pace to them. This hymn (GGS: 599) has 4 stanzas, is the 1st in the third *gharu* style of Sorath raga, 12th in the sequence, identified as 4:1:12.

DHANASARI RAGA

66 Dhanasari raga (GGS: 660–695) opens with Guru Nanak's poem that forms a part of the "Thousand Words," a morning hymn. Guru Nanak's *Āratī* hymn (see Glossary) is also composed in Dhanasari raga.

67 This hymn (GGS: 661-662), identified as 4:3:5, has 4 stanzas, is 3rd in the second *gharu* style of Dhanasari raga, and 5th in the sequence. The next two hymns follow it sequentially.

68 This verse has also been translated as "at His Command, the wind blows everywhere" (*www.srigranth.org*).

69 Everybody is saved; there are no "elect."

70 Written from the beginning of creation.

71 Alludes to the three strands: truth, passion, and inertia.

72 This hymn follows the sequence of the preceding ones. It is 1st in the third *gharu* style of Dhanasari raga.

73 Guru Nanak is referring to yogic breathing techniques that control inhalation and exhalation.

74 I wonder if the word *aloa* ("odd"), used to describe the lotus position, is a pun on the *anuloma* breath exercises.

75 Allusion to the Mughal rulers.

76 The "eight adornments" (in the original *asaṭa sāju*) are the rules of recitation, interpretation, or grammar (Shackle 1981: 45).

77 This composition is followed by Guru Nanak's evening hymn.

78 GGS: 685.

79 "Masters," original *nāthu,* retains the yogi context of the passage.

80 The subject is not stated explicitly. It could be truth itself, but most likely Guru Nanak is referring to the guru-facing who embody truth. In his dialogue with the siddhas he explicitly states, "truth and true beings are one and the same" (stanza 25).

TILANG RAGA

81 Tilang raga (GGS: 721–727) was widespread among the Sufis, and, in consonance with its musical context, Guru Nanak's hymns are saturated with Sufi expressions. Starting with the first word "*yaka*" (number "one" in Persian), this whole poem is in a form of "spoken Persian," with only a handful of vernacular words. The first four hymns of Tilang raga are translated here. They follow sequentially (GGS:721–722), but they are set in different *gharu* styles of Tilang raga.

82 All four terms for God in this verse are Islamic: *Hakku* (Arabic *ḥaqq*, true), *Kabīra* (great), *Karīma* (merciful), and *Parvadagāru* (sustainer).

83 Angel of death in Islam.

84 *Takabīra,* Muslim proclamation of the greatness of God, recited at funerals.

85 Longing for the divine is here couched in *samā* aesthetic, which was popular among Chishti Sufis to produce religious emotion and ecstasy. However, the rich Sufi significance in Guru Nanak's poetics is glossed over by exegetes and translators. For discussion, see N. G. K. Singh 2019: 33–55.

86 Guru Nanak's question brings to mind, "Who is better than Allah at coloring" (Qur'an, Sura 2: 138).

87 "With brothers," *sabharāī.* In the patriarchal society of the Panjab, a sister with brothers is considered lucky, as opposed to the one who has none. Also, a reminder of her natal family.

SUHI RAGA

88 The term "*sūhā*" (crimson) symbolizes the joyful state of brides (*suhāgaṇi*) and grooms (*suhāga*), and Guru Nanak's hymns explore this exalted mode of existence from different angles. In his Suhi compositions, we get to see weddings conducted with pomp and ceremony, and we hear the wondrous symphony of timeless music. "The Graceless" and "The Graceful" in the preceding section also are set in Suhi raga. This hymn (GGS: 730), identified as 4:1:8, has

4 stanzas, is 1st in the seventh *gharu* style of Suhi raga, and 8th in the sequence. The next, identified as 4:2:9, follows its sequence.

89   *Lālu* in the original signifies ruby, red, precious, love.

90   GGS: 765.

91   The five senses (implied) are in tune with the sacred word.

92   "Enlightened," *avrītā*, literally, "unveiled." According to *Mahān Koś*, "whose veil of ignorance has been removed" (1960: 66).

93   "Arena" (*piṛu*), a wrestling pitch to overcome vices.

94   The image of stirring evokes a circular meditative gesture in mystic experience.

BILAVAL RAGA

95   "Sir," *mīāṁ*.

96   Expressive of joy, Bilaval raga ("delight") is associated with the spring season (GGS: 795–858). Guru Nanak's hymns in this measure transmit the zesty taste of the divine name. His composition "The Days of the Lunar Month" (section 4) also is in Bilaval raga.

97   Guru Nanak strikingly uses the feminine form Sahibā, "sovereign lady" or "queen."

98   These two hymns set at the opening of Bilaval raga are also a part of the morning prayer "Thousand Words."

99   Reference to illusion (*māyā*).

100   Eight-stanza hymn, GGS: 832.

101   Depiction of an upper-class Brahman who wears a clean loincloth, and a holy dot and necklace.

MARU RAGA

102   The word "*mārū*" is derived from *mārūsthala* (dry land), and so the heat of the searing desert is evoked in Guru Nanak's verse recorded in this raga (GGS: 989–1106). Maru is the only raga in the GGS where we find sixteen-stanza hymns (*solāhā*).

103   GGS: 990.

104   "Going off," *galiā*, literally means "rotting."

105   Reference to lust, anger, greed, attachment, and pride.

106   *Āgamas* are sacred literature belonging to various traditions including the Shiva, Vishnu, Goddess, Jain, and Buddhist. They describe liturgy and contain detailed information about the construction of temples and the making of divine images.

107 For murmur, see *japu* in the Glossary.

108 GGS: 991.

109 "Off-key," *betālā* (*be*/off + *tāla*/musical beat), somebody not restricted by societal prescriptions. Later Sufi poet Bullhe Shah uses the same word: "Those touched by perfect love dance out of tune (*besura*), they dance out of step (*betāla*)." For more see (N. G. K. Singh 2012: 96).

110 The first of the sixteen-stanza hymns (GGS: 1020).

111 Reminiscent of the epilogue of the "Morning Hymn," the opening hymn of the GGS.

112 *Bhogī*, one who enjoys. Also section 4, n. 65.

113 Hearts savoring the sacred word are so powerful that facing them, death and birth "go insane" (*bhae devāne*). This interesting Nanakian image is glossed over by most exegetes, but Sahib Singh notes it in his commentary (1962: GGS, 1021).

114 Evokes the cosmic bull holding the weight of the earth. In stanza 16 of his "Morning Hymn" Guru Nanak explains, "The bull that bears the earth is righteousness, child of compassion."

115 Again, the five thieves are the negative psychic forces of lust (*kāma*), anger (*krodha*), greed (*lobhu*), attachment (*mohu*), and pride (*ahaṁkāru*), which rob people of their authentic selfhood.

116 Guru Nanak describes the sacred Hindu places: the river Ganga; the river Jamuna on whose banks Krishna sang and danced with his cowherd friends; and Kedara, a pilgrimage site in the Himalayas, sacred to Shiva.

117 In this segment of the verse, Guru Nanak mentions several holy cities in different corners of the Indian subcontinent by name: Kashi, Kanchivaram, Puri, and Dwarka, indicative of his theological vision of an all-inclusive, vast, bustling, infinite reality.

118 This hymn, identified as 16:3:15, has 16 stanzas, is 3rd in the Deccani style of Maru raga, and 15th in the sequence (GGS: 1035-1036).

119 *"Jati-satī,"* lit. celibates and virtuous women.

120 "Comfort" (*sukha*) "dwellers" (*vāsī*) suggest house owners (different from the forest dwellers).

121 *Jaṅgam* are a Shaiva order of wandering ascetics.

122 Allusion to Krishna.

123 While Gorakhnath was the reputed founder of the *nātha* sect of yogis, Matsyendra is believed to have received the sacred teachings

directly from Shiva, which he then passed on to his premier student Gorakhnath. Besides the order of the *nāthas,* Matsyendra is also closely associated with the Buddhist Vajrayana tradition.

124 *Homa* (libation) and *jagu* (Skt. *yajña,* sacrifice) for the Vedic ritual of making offerings in the fire.

125 Guru Nanak presents a kaleidoscopic view of the Hindu world— the social classes including the Brahmans (priests and scholars) and Kshatriyas (warriors and kings), the Vedic rituals of making offerings in the fire, multiple gods, temples, the most sacred Gayatri verse in the *Ṛg Veda* (3.62.10), making pilgrimages, bathing at holy sites, and so on.

126 This verse projects the Islamic world, including the religious specialists in charge of a mosque (mullah), judges in courts of Islamic law (*qazis*), Sufi Masters (shaikhs), Muslim holy men (*masāiku*), devotees who make the pilgrimage to Mecca (*hājī*), and Muslim rulers and their subjects.

BHAIRON RAGA

127 Bhairon raga is described as an awe-inspiring musical melody, and Guru Nanak's hymns with their awesome beauty are appropriately framed in it. It constitutes pp. 1125–1167 of the GGS.

128 This hymn, identified as 4:2:3, has 4 stanzas, is 2nd in the second *gharu* style of Bhairon raga, and 3rd in the sequence.

BASANT RAGA

129 Guru Nanak's festive greeting, "*mumārakhī*" (from Arabic *mubārak*), a common term for "congratulations," is an instant mnemonic of the beneficent current (*barakā*) flowing through the arteries of the cosmos.

130 Basant is the raga of spring (Sanskrit *vasanta*), GGS: 1168–1196, and for Guru Nanak the sensuous spring blossoms are but a burst of the glorious universal current.

131 "Creative power" (*kudarati*) defined as the nature and power of the divine. For more see stanza 3:2 in the "Ballad in the Melody of Hope" (section 2).

132 Hari is not specified in the original, only implied in "*hare*" (green).

133 Touching the feet is a South Asian gesture of reverence.

134 The complete cycle of sixty years consists of three twenty-year periods named after the Hindu trinity, Brahma, Vishnu, and Shiva (Enthoven 1989: 80).

135 Cultural expression for honoring.

136 The "four lines" (*caunkā*) are drawn to form a square that circumscribes the sacred area in the kitchen.

137 The "ten plus eight" are the eighteen Sanskrit Puranas.

138 Almsgiving depending on the different castes.

139 GGS: 1169.

140 This passage reveals Guru Nanak's equation of yoga of "serenity" (*sahaj*) with yoga of "devotion" (*bhakti*). Also section 2, n. 16.

141 An aniconic representation of preserver god Vishnu in the form of a black fossil shell, found in the river Gandaki.

142 Basil is considered to be holy in Hindu practice.

143 This poem and the next two are set in Basant Hindol raga. The springtime melody (Basant) is aptly combined with the sprightly tree swings (*hiṇḍol*).

144 The Persian wheel is a mechanical water-lifting device in which a number of buckets are attached to a long chain. Two gear wheels make up the system, operated by animals like bullocks, buffaloes, or camels.

145 "Natal home and in-laws' home" is a metaphor for this life and beyond, frequently used by Sufi poets.

146 The bride makes a distinction between the "written syllables" (*akharu likhai*), an account of her own actions, and the "holy verse" (*bāṇī*) revealed by the guru, which could free her.

147 The "two syllables" (*dui akharu*) most likely imply the "true name" (*satu nāmu*).

148 When trapped in dualisms, the mind rules over a flimsy body, unable to comprehend the universal reality.

149 Gold is measured in *tolās* and *māsās* (12 *māsās* = 1 *tolā*), therefore "*tolā* one minute, and *māsā* another" is a common expression for a capricious personality.

150 GGS: 1187.

151 Literally "fat," *moṭau*.

152 "One religion" in the original is *eko dharamu*.

153 "One being," *ekkoaṅkāra* (*ikkoaṅkāra*).

154 "Guests," *mahimānu*, of the divine host.

155 GGS: 1190.

156 *Kaṁvalu*, "lotus" is "*maya*" for Taran Singh (1969: 1331) and Gopal Singh (1978: 1140); Lakshmi for Talib (1984–90: 2404).

157 The original for "unborn" is *akulu*, without family and relatives. Also, section 3, n. 41.

PRABHATI RAGA

158 The penultimate Prabhati ("shining forth") is a morning raga
(GGS: 1327–1351). The Prabhati conveys the intensity of Nanak's
spiritual desire through the morning activities of dressing up and
milking cows, while the Persian wheel (n. 144 above) continues to
gurgle in the background.

159 GGS: 1329.

160 GGS: 1330.

161 Reference to the five lower passions.

162 The image of a fetus turned upside down in the uterus alludes to
rebirth, the continuation of the cycle of reincarnation.

163 The result of prior actions.

164 "Slips and flaws" in the original are echo words *bhulu cuku*.

165 In the term *ravindā*, Nanak brings together the illumination of the
sun (*ravi*) and moon (*indu*). See also Gopal Singh (1978: 1268).

GLOSSARY

āgamas sacred literature belonging to various Indic traditions; contain detailed information on liturgy, the construction of temples, and the making of divine images

AIPANTH one of the twelve sects of yogis who worship Ai Bhavani, a primeval mother goddess

akharu words

ALĀHṆĪĀṄ Songs of Mourning

ALLAH God; name for the divine

ānandu transcendent bliss

ĀRATĪ evening hymn of worship

baba (*bābā*) an endearing term for an older man

BĀBARVĀṆĪ four hymns composed by Guru Nanak on Emperor Babur's defeat of the Lodi Sultans, and the establishment of the Mughal Empire in 1526

bāṇī holy verse; also called *gurbāṇī*, the guru's holy utterance; a single hymn or the whole of the Guru Granth Sahib is known as *bāṇī* or *gurbāṇī*

BRAHMA creator god

chhant lyrical composition of four or more stanzas of six lines

darśan "to see," in the Sikh context, being in the presence of the Guru Granth Sahib

dervish Muslim mendicant

DHARNIDHAR holder of the earth, name for the non-incarnate divine

DHRUVA committed devotees, unchanging like the Pole Star

durūd blessings recited for the Prophet Muhammad

GĀYATRĪ MANTRA the most sacred verse in the *Ṛg Veda* (3.62.10), also referred to as the "three-versed"

gharu "house," a musical style in which a hymn of a particular raga is performed

GURDWĀRĀ sacred space of the Sikhs, with the Guru Granth Sahib at its center

gurmukhi guru-facing, opposite of the *manmukhi* (the egotistical "self-facing"); the *gurmukhi* live in harmony with the universal divine

GURMUKHĪ "from the mouth of the guru," the script in which Guru Nanak's verses and those of his successors are recorded in the Guru Granth Sahib

guru a channel for awakening the consciousness to the divine reality; generally a teacher or enlightener; Guru Nanak is the first of the ten historical gurus in the Sikh religion

GURU GRANTH the scripture of the Sikhs, respectfully called the Guru Granth Sahib

hājī Muslim who makes the pilgrimage to Mecca

HAQQ "truth," name for the divine

HARI "the tawny one," name for the non-incarnate divine

haumai selfish ego, literally "I-me," which divides the person from their essential oneness with the divine, the cosmos, and their society

hukamu divine will or order; everything physical, psychological, cosmic, and spiritual depends on it

ikkoaṅkār "one being," the fundamental Sikh expression for the divine

INDRA the king of the gods in Hindu mythology

JAGJIVAN life of the universe; name for the divine

janamsākhīs narratives about the birth and life of Guru Nanak

jaṅgam Shaivite wandering ascetic

japu murmuring a text, reciting it to yourself

JAPUJĪ the inaugural composition in the Guru Granth Sahib, recited daily in the morning by the devout

KABIR (*kabīra*) "great," name for the divine

karamu human actions and their results, which either win freedom from the circle of birth and death or trap the doer in that circle

KARIM (*karīma*) "merciful," name for the divine

KATEB the four sacred books of the Semitic tradition: the holy Qur'an, the Tawrut (Torah), the Zabur (Psalms), and the Injil (Gospel)

KHUDA (*khudā*) "God," name for the divine

kudarati nature and power of the divine

lekhā "writ," an all-embracing written law that governs the existence and movement of the multiverse

mahalā term used with a numeral to identify authorship in the *Guru Granth Sahib*

manne the state of embracing the divine by the heart or mind

manu mind or heart

masāiku (*mashāikhs*) Muslim legal scholars

MAULA "master," "protector," name for the divine

māyā "illusion," represents the false qualities of the world, e.g., its supposed permanence and durability

mūla mantru prelude to Guru Nanak's *japujī*; it is the foundational belief of the Sikh faith

mullah religious specialist in charge of a mosque

MURARI "destroyer of demons," an epithet of god Krishna, who destroys the demon Mūrā

nāda numinous sound

namaz Islamic daily prayer

nāmu "name," the expression of the nature and being of the divine

nātha "protector," also used as a general term for a master or leader and for the order of *nātha* yogis, who trace their lineage to Adinath, their original master Lord Shiva

paharu about a three-hour period; in the Indian time frame, night and day were each divided into four quarters or watches (*pahare*)

PARAMESARU "supreme ruler," name for the divine

PARVADAGARU "provider," "sustainer," name for the divine

PAṬĪ LIKHĪ "alphabet on the wooden board," Guru Nanak's acrostic composed in Āsā melody

pauṛī staircase, and a general word for "stanza" in the longer scriptural compositions

pīr Muslim saint

PRABHU (also PRABH and PRABHI) "powerful one," name for the divine

prakāś "bring to light," the morning ritual of opening of the Guru Granth Sahib

PRANADHARA "upholder of life or breath," name for the divine

PURAKHU (*puruśa*) person; the timeless, infinite being

PURANAS (*Purāṇas*) the eighteen Hindu holy books that recount the deeds of the gods

qazi (*qāzī*) judge of Islamic law

RABB "sustainer," name for the divine

raga a series of five or more notes upon which a melody is based

ragini female counterpart of the male raga; across North India in the sixteenth century, ragas were represented in human form both aurally and visually

rahāu pause; most hymns in the GGS include a special verse that carries the central theme and ends with the word *rahāu*

RAHIM (*rahīma*) "the merciful," name for the non-incarnate divine

raṅga color, pleasure

rasa juice, quintessential joy

śabadu "sacred word," the divine revelation; also used for a scriptural hymn

sahaj "serenity," a natural and spontaneous state of oneness and freedom when actions and thoughts emerge effortlessly, without the pull of the dualistic "I-me"

SAHIB "lord," name for the non-incarnate divine

SAHIBA "sovereign lady," name for the non-incarnate divine

sairu (*shā'ir*) poet

SAMĀ Sufi union with the divine through sacred music and dance

satu nāmu "true name," the real name of the divine is truth; all others are only aspects of truth

shaikhs Sufi Masters

shastras (*śāstras*) "treatises" include the many books of Hinduism that provide religious, scientific, philosophical, moral, poetic, and architectural instruction

siddhas "accomplished," refers to the eighty-four mystics believed to have attained immortality through the practice of yoga

siṅṅī horn blown by yogis

smṛtīs "remembered," these are the twenty-seven collections of Hindu law and ceremony

solāhā sixteen-stanza hymns

SRIRANGA "splendid-colored," name for the non-incarnate divine

sucajī a graceful or competent woman; her antithesis is the *kucajī* (ungraceful or incompetent); also the title of the poem by Guru Nanak

SUFI practitioner of the mystical dimension of Islam

suhāgaṇi a happy wife

sunnu (Sanskrit *śūnya*) term for the divine without any attributes

THITĪṄ "The Dates," Guru Nanak's composition based on the monthly cycle of the lunar days

tulasī the sacred basil plant

vār a heroic ode

VASUDEVA "Indwelling god," name for the non-incarnate divine

VEDA the four foundational scriptures of Hinduism: *Ṛg, Yajur, Sāma,* and *Atharva;* also used by Guru Nanak as a general term for "knowledge"

vismādu "wonder," the feeling of wonder evoked by the beauty and vastness of creation; the dominant aesthetic mood in Guru Nanak's poetics

Numbers with Special Significance

1 *ikku* expression of unity; refers to the absolute being

1¼ *savā* an expression of abundance

2 *dūjā* "duality," sense of I/me/mine that divides the individual from the universal one

3 *trai* three could refer to:
  traiguṇa the three strands governing worldly existence (*sattva, rajas,* and *tamas*)
  trailoka the three worlds: celestial, terrestrial, and nether worlds
  traipāla the three-lined verse, the *Gāyatrī*

4 *cāri* four could refer to:
  cāre khaṇī the four sources of life (born of egg, womb, earth, and sweat)
  cāre kuṇṭa the four quarters
  cāre Veda the four Vedas
  cavgaṇi "fourfold," common expression for great joy
  cauthā pada "fourth stage," could refer either to the Upanishadic ideal of "*turiyā*" (the fourth and final stage of liberation) or to the Sufi ideal of gnosis (*ma'rifat*), the fourth and final stage of the Sufi path

5 *pañca* refers to the five senses that can be honed into the virtues of truth (*satu*), contentment (*santokhu*), morality (*dharamu*), compassion (*daiā*), and

patience (*dhīraju*); conversely, they can degenerate into five psychological afflictions, lust (*kāma*), anger (*krodhu*), greed (*lobhu*), attachment (*mohu*), and pride (*ahaṁkāru*)

6 *chia* refers to the six philosophical systems of Samkhya, Yoga, Nyaya, Vaisheshika, Mimamsa, and Vedanta

7 *sata* or *sāta* as in *sāta samunda,* the five senses, plus mind and consciousness

8 *aṭha* as in the "watches" (*pahare*) of the day in the Indian time system; also refers to the eight *siddhi* powers: to make one's body smaller than the smallest (*aṇimā*), greater than the greatest (*mahimā*), lighter than the lightest (*laghimā*), heavier than the heaviest (*garimā*), the power to acquire everything (*prāpti*),

the power to experience every joy (*prakāmya*), superiority over all (*īśitvā*), and mastery over the self (*vaśitvā*)

9 *nava* nine could refer to:
navaghara nine openings of the human body
navakhaṇda nine climate zones; the whole earth
navanidhi nine great treasures; popular term for all the treasures in this world

10 *dasa* ten could refer to:
dasam duāra the tenth door; it opens at the finale of the yogic process
dasvai tenth; refers to the part of the human body that leads to divine consciousness

18 *aṭhāraha* 8 +10, the eighteen Puranas

68 *aṭhasaṭhi* 8 + 60, the sixty-eight sacred sites of India

BIBLIOGRAPHY

Editions and Translations

Dass, Nirmal. 2000. *Songs of the Saints from the Adi Granth: Translation and Introduction.* Albany: State University of New York Press.

Gurbilās Chevviṅ Pātsāhī. 1970. Patiala: Punjab Languages Department.

Macauliffe, Max Arthur. 1909 (reprint 1963). *The Sikh Religion: Its Gurus, Sacred Writings and Authors.* 6 vols. Oxford: Oxford University Press.

Mandair, Arvind and C. Shackle, ed. and trans. 2005. *Teachings of the Sikh Gurus: Selections from the Sikh Scriptures.* London, New York: Routledge.

McLeod, W. H. 1984. *Textual Sources for the Study of Sikhism.* Chicago: University of Chicago Press.

Śabadārath Sri Guru Granth Sāhibjī. Vols. 1–4. 1969. Amritsar: Shiromani Gurdwara Prabandhak Committee.

Singh, Bhai Jodh. 1968. *Śrī Kartarpurī Bīṛ de Darśan.* Patiala: Punjabi University

Singh, Bhai Vir. 1958–1962. *Saṅthyā rī Gurū Granth Sāhib.* 7 vols. Amritsar: Khalsa Samacar.

——— 1981. *Japujī Sāhib Saṅthyā.* Amritsar: Khalsa Samacar.

———, ed. 1948. *Purātan Janamsākhī Srī Gurū Nānak Dev Jī.* Amritsar: Khalsa Samachar.

———, ed. 1977. *Vārāṅ Bhai Gurdas.* Amritsar: Khalsa Samachar.

Singh, Gopal. 1960. *Sri Guru Granth Sahib: English Version.* 4 vols. Delhi: Gurdas Kapur. Reprint, Chandigarh: World Sikh University Press, 1978.

Singh, Kartar. 1996. *Japujī Sāhib te hor baṇīā dā sṭīk.* Amritsar: Shiromani Gurdwara Prabhandak Committee.

Singh, Khushwant and Arpita Singh. 1991. *Hymns of Guru Nanak.* Hyderabad: Orient Longman.

Singh, Manmohan. 1962–1969. *Sri Guru Granth Sahib.* 8 vols. (with text and transliteration). Amritsar: Shiromani Gurdwara Parbandhak Committee.

Singh, Nikky-Guninder Kaur. 1995. *The Name of My Beloved: Verses of the Sikh Gurus.* New York: HarperCollins. Reprint, New Delhi: Penguin, 2001.

————2012. *Of Sacred and Secular Desire: An Anthology of Lyrical Writings from the Punjab.* London: I.B. Tauris.

————2019. *The Hymns of the Sikh Gurus.* New Delhi: Penguin Classics.

Singh, Sahib. *Śrī Gurū Granth Sāhib Darapaṇ.* Text of the GGS and full commentary in 10 volumes. 1962–1964. Panjab: Jullundur. Electronically available by GGS pages: www.srigranth.org.

Singh, Santokh. 1844. *Śrī Gur Pratap Sūraj Granth Rās 3.* Digitized by Baljinder Singh, 16914 Lassen Street, Northridge, Calif.

Singh, Taran, ed. 1969. *Gurū Nānak Bāṇī Prakāś.* Vols. 1 & 2. Patiala: Punjabi University.

Singh, Trilochan et al. 1960. *Selections from the Sacred Writings of the Sikhs.* London: George Allen & Unwin.

Talib, G. S. 1977. *Japuji: The Immortal Prayer-Chant.* New Delhi: Munshiram Manoharlal Publishers.

————1984–1990. *Sri Guru Granth Sahib: An English Translation.* 4 vols. Patiala: Punjabi University.

Trumpp, Ernest. 1877. *The Adi Granth or The Holy Scriptures of the Sikhs.* London: George Allen & Unwin. Reprint, New Delhi: Munshiram Manoharlal Publishers, 1978.

Other Sources

Ādi Śrī Guru Granth Sāhibjī Stīk (Faridkot Vālā Ṭīkā). 4 vols. 1970. Patiala: Punjab Languages Department.

Aijazuddin, F. S. 1979. *Sikh Portraits by European Artists.* London, New York: Sotheby Parke Bernet.

Alter, Robert. 2019. *The Hebrew Bible.* New York: Norton.

Beveridge, H. 1897–1939. *The Akbarnama of Abu-L-Fazl.* Vol. III. Translated from the Persian. Calcutta: The Asiatic Society.

Bruijn, Thomas de and Allison Busch. 2014. *Culture and Circulation: Literatures in Motion in Early Modern India.* Leiden, Boston: Brill.

Callewaert, Winand M. 1996. *Śrī Guru Granth Sāhib with Complete Index.* New Delhi: Motilal Banarsidass Publishers.

Curtiss, Marie Joy. 1996. "Gurmat Saṅgīt." In *Encyclopedia of Sikhism,* ed. Harbans Singh. Patiala: Punjabi University.

Dass, Hari. 2008. *Yoga Sutras of Patanjali: A Study Guide for Book II.* Santa Cruz: Sri Rama Publishing.

Deol, Jeevan. 2001. "Text and Lineage in Early Sikh History: Issues in the Study of the Adi Granth." *Bulletin of the School of Oriental and African Studies,* University of London 64, 1: 34–58.

————2003. "Illustration and Illumination in Sikh Scriptural Manuscripts." In *New Insights into Sikh Art,* ed. Kavita Singh. Mumbai: Marg Publications.

Enthoven, R. E. 1989. *Folklore of Gujarat* from the Folklore Notes collected by AMT Jackson. Vol. 1. New Delhi: Asian Educational Services.

Goswamy, B. N. 2000. *Piety and Splendour: Sikh Heritage in Art.* New Delhi: National Museum.

Goswamy, B. N. and Caron Smith. 2006. *I See No Stranger: Early Sikh Art and Devotion.* New York: Rubin Museum of Art.

Hans, Surjit. 1987. *B-40 Janamsakhi Guru Baba Nanak Paintings.* Amritsar: Guru Nanak Dev University.

Hopkins, Antony. 1977. *Talking about Music: Symphonies, Concertos and Sonatas.* London and Sydney: Pan Books.

Hortsman, Monika. 2015. "The Example in Dadupanthi Homiletics." In *Tellings and Texts: Music, Literature and Performance in North India,* ed. F. Orsini et al. Cambridge: Open Book Publishers, pp. 31–59.

Inden, Ronald B., Jonathan S. Walters, and Daud Ali. 2000. *Querying the Medieval: Texts and the History of Practice in South Asia.* Cary, N.C., USA: Oxford University Press.

Khalsa, Sant Singh. "Sri Granth." Accessed January 12, 2021. www.srigranth.org.

KhojGurbani. "KhojGurbani." Accessed January 12, 2021. https://www.khojgurbani.org/home.

Kohli, S. S. 1961. *A Critical Study of the Adi Granth.* New Delhi: Punjabi Writers Cooperative.

Linden, Bob van der. 2013. "Sikh Sacred Music: Identity, Aesthetics, and Historical Change." In *Music and Empire in Britain and India,* ed. B. Linden. New York: Palgrave Macmillan, pp. 129–156.

————2015. "Pre-Twentieth-Century Sikh Sacred Music: The Mughals, Courtly Patronage and Canonisation." *South Asia: Journal of South Asian Studies* 38, 2: 141–155.

Macauliffe, M. A. 1880. "Diwali at Amritsar." *Calcutta Review,* Calcutta, LXXI, 1880: 257–272.

Mann, Gurinder Singh. 1997. *Goindval Pothis: The Earliest Extant Source of the Sikh Canon.* Cambridge, Mass.: Harvard University Press.

————2001. *The Making of Sikh Scripture.* New York: Oxford University Press.

283

McLeod, W. H. 1968. *Guru Nanak and the Sikh Religion*. Oxford: Clarendon.

———1980. *Early Sikh Tradition: A Study of the Janam-sakhis*. Oxford: Clarendon Press.

Melton, J. Gordon. 2011. *Religious Celebrations: An Encyclopedia of Holidays, Festivals, Solemn Observances and Spiritual Commemorations*. Santa Barbara, Denver, Oxford: ABC-CLIO.

Myrvold, Kristina. 2010. "Making the Scripture a Person: Reinventing Death Rituals of Guru Granth Sahib in Sikhism." In *The Death of Sacred Texts: Ritual Disposal and Renovation of Texts in World Religions*, ed. K. Myrvold. London and New York: Routledge, pp. 125–146.

Nayar, Kamla and Jaswinder Singh Sandhu. 2007. *The Socially Involved Renunciate: Guru Nānak's Discourse to the Nāth Yogis*. Albany: State University of New York Press.

Nijhawan, Michael. 2003. "From Divine Bliss to Ardent Passion: Exploring Sikh Religious Aesthetics through the Ḍhāḍī." *History of Religions* 42, 4: 359–385.

———2006. *Dhadi Darbar: Religion, Violence, and the Performance of Sikh History*. New Delhi: Oxford University Press.

Novetzke, Christian Lee. 2008. *Religion and Public Memory: A Cultural History of Saint Namdev in India*. New York: Columbia University Press.

Oberoi, Harjot. 1994. *The Construction of Religious Boundaries: Culture, Identity, and Diversity in the Sikh Tradition*. Chicago: University of Chicago Press.

Orsini, Francesca, ed. 2006. *Love in South Asia: A Cultural History*. Cambridge: Cambridge University Press.

———2015. "Texts and Tellings: Kathas in the Fifteenth and Sixteenth Centuries." In *Tellings and Texts: Music, Literature and Performance in North India*, ed. F. Orsini et al. Cambridge: Open Book Publishers, pp. 327–357.

———2018. "Clouds, Cuckoos and an Empty Bed: Emotions in Hindi-Urdu Barahmasas." In *Monsoon Feelings: A History of Emotions in the Rain*, ed. Imke Rajamani, Margrit Pernau, and Katherine Butler Schofield. New Delhi: Niyogi Books.

Pauwels, Heidi. 2010. "Are the Enemies of the Bhaktas? Testimony about 'Saktas' and 'Others' from Kabir, the Ramanandis, Tulsidas, and Hariram Vyas." *Journal of the American Oriental Society* 130, 4: 509–539.

Phillips, Stephen H. 2009. *Yoga, Karma, and Rebirth: A Brief History and Philosophy.* New York: Columbia University Press.

Pincott, Frederic. 1886. "The Arrangement of the Hymns of the Adi Granth." *Journal of the Royal Asiatic Society of Great Britain & Ireland* 18, 3: 437–461.

Ramey, Steven. 2013. "Liminal Hindus: Disputed Boundaries and Their Impacts on Sindhi Hindus." In *Lines in Water: Religious Boundaries South Asia,* ed. E. Kent et al. Syracuse, N.Y.: Syracuse University Press.

Rogers, Alexander, trans., and Henry Beveridge, ed. 1909. *Memories of Jahangir.* London: Royal Asiatic Society.

Rose, Horace Arthur, Denzil Ibbetson, and Edward Maclagan. Reprint 1990. *Glossary of the Tribes and Castes of the Punjab and North West Frontier Province.* New Delhi, Madras: Asian Educational Services. Original edition, 1919.

Schimmel, Annemarie. 2004. *The Empire of the Great Mughals: History, Art and Culture.* London: Reaktion Books.

———2011. "Color Symbolism in Persian Literature" in Encyclopedia Iranica, *http://www.iranicaonline.org/articles/color-pers-rang.*

Shackle, C. 1981. *A Guru Nanak Glossary.* London: School of Oriental and African Studies.

———1983. *An Introduction to the Sacred Language of the Sikhs.* London: School of Oriental and African Studies.

———1988. "Some Observations on the Evolution of Modern Standard Punjabi." In *Sikh History and Religion in the Twentieth Century,* ed. J. T. O'Connell, M. Israel, and W. G. Oxtoby. Toronto: University of Toronto, Centre for South Asian Studies.

SikhRi."The Guru Granth Sahib Project." Accessed Janary 12, 2021. https://app.gurugranthsahib.io.

Singh, Avtar. 1970. *Ethics of the Sikhs.* Patiala: Punjabi University.

Singh, Ganda, ed. 1962. *Early European Accounts of the Sikhs.* Reprint: *Indian Studies: Past and Present.* Calcutta: A. Guha.

———1976. "Baba Farid—A Real Saint." *In Socio-Cultural Impact of Islam on India,* ed. Attar Singh. Chandigarh: Panjab University.

Singh, Harbans. 1969. *Guru Nanak and Origins of the Sikh Faith.* Bombay: Asia Publishing House.

———1985. *The Heritage of the Sikhs.* New Delhi: Manohar Publications.

———1988. *Sri Guru Granth Sahib: The Guru Eternal for the Sikhs.* Patiala: Academy of Sikh Religion and Culture.

———1992–1998. *Encyclopedia of Sikhism.* Patiala: Punjabi University.

Singh, Nikky-Guninder Kaur. 1992. "The Sikh Bridal Symbol: An Epiphany of Interconnections." *Journal of Feminist Studies in Religion* 8, 2: 41–64.

———1993. *The Feminine Principle in the Sikh Vision of the Transcendent.* Cambridge: Cambridge University Press.

———2005. *The Birth of the Khalsa: A Feminist Re-Memory of Sikh Identity.* Albany: State University of New York Press.

———2007. "Translating Sikh Scripture into English." *Sikh Formations* 3, 1: 33–49.

———2008. "Guru Granth: The Quintessential Sikh Metaphor." *Postscripts: The Journal of Sacred Texts & Contemporary Worlds* 4, 2: 157–176.

———2013. "Corporeal Metaphysics: Guru Nanak in Early Sikh Art." *History of Religions* 53, 1: 28–65.

———2017. "Sikh Mysticism and Sensuous Reproductions." In *Ineffability: An Exercise in Comparative Philosophy of Religion*, ed. T. Knepper and L. Kalmanson. Cham, Switzerland: Springer International, pp. 113–134.

———2017. "M.A. Macauliffe and the Angst of the Translator." *Journal of the Irish Society for the Academic Study of Religions* 4: 33–57.

———2019. *The First Sikh: The Life and Legacy of Guru Nanak.* New Delhi: Penguin Random House.

Singh, Pashaura. 2000. *The Guru Granth: Canon, Meaning and Authority.* New Delhi: Oxford University Press.

——— 2003. *The Bhagats of the Guru Granth Sahib.* New Delhi: Oxford University Press.

Smith, Brian. 1986. "Ritual, Knowledge, and Being." *Numen* 33, 1.

Stoler Miller, Barbara. 1977. *Love Song of the Dark Lord: Jayadeva's Gītagovinda.* New York: Columbia University Press.

Thackston, Wheeler M., ed. and trans. 1996. *The Baburnāmā: Memoirs of Babur, Prince and Emperor.* Oxford: Oxford University Press, in association with the Smithsonian Institute.